Manufacturing Dissent

Single-issue protest, the public and the press

Kirsty Milne

DEMCS

About Demos

Demos is a greenhouse for new ideas which can improve the quality of our lives. As an independent think tank, we aim to create an open resource of knowledge and learning that operates beyond traditional party politics.

We connect researchers, thinkers and practitioners to an international network of people changing politics. Our ideas regularly influence government policy, but we also work with companies, NGOs, colleges and professional bodies.

Demos knowledge is organised around five themes, which combine to create new perspectives. The themes are democracy, learning, enterprise, quality of life and global change.

But we also understand that thinking by itself is not enough. Demos has helped to initiate a number of practical projects which are delivering real social benefit through the redesign of public services.

We bring together people from a wide range of backgrounds to cross-fertilise ideas and experience. By working with Demos, our partners develop a sharper insight into the way ideas shape society. For Demos, the process is as important as the final product.

www.demos.co.uk

First published in 2005
© Demos
Some rights reserved – see copyright licence for details

ISBN 1 84180 141 0
Typeset by Land & Unwin, Bugbrooke
Printed by HenDI Systems, London

For further information and
subscription details please contact:

Demos
Magdalen House
136 Tooley Street
London SE1 2TU

telephone: 0845 458 5949
email: hello@demos.co.uk
web: www.demos.co.uk

Contents

	Acknowledgements	7
1.	Introduction: press-protest comes of age	9
2.	Protest: from footprint to newsprint	13
3.	Case studies: the press on the picket line	21
	Paedophiles, Paulsgrove and the *News of the World*	22
	Freedom and the price of petrol	27
	Gay sex lessons from the *Daily Record*	35
4.	The new opposition?	43
5.	Referendum-itis	48
6.	Giving voice, shrinking space	56
7.	Manufacturing dissent: press and parties in transition	63
	Notes	72

Acknowledgements

I would like to thank the Nieman Foundation at Harvard University, where this pamphlet was conceived; the Center for European Studies, where it was written; and the Fulbright Commission in London. I am grateful for advice and inspiration from Patricia Craig, Peter Hall, John Lloyd, Louise Richardson, Michael Sandel, John Tomaney, Stefaan Walgrave and Stewart Wood. Special thanks to Hugh Shaw Stewart for his encouragement.

1. Introduction: press-protest comes of age

There is an opposition in this country: it just isn't the one we recognise.

A paradox pervades British public life. On the one hand, falling electoral turnout and a crisis of trust in party politics. On the other, surges of single-issue protest over subjects such as fuel prices, foxhunting and the war in Iraq. These suggest that, far from being apathetic, voters have interests which diverge from the standard political agenda and are seeking other outlets to express them. The implications of this growing divide will only be clear if we understand a new phenomenon: the conjunction of media power and popular protest that is reshaping the terms of political engagement.

Received wisdom holds that the people are giving up on politics and heading for the exit. During the 2001 UK general election there was a turnout of just 59 per cent, the lowest since 1918, prompting a committee of MPs to diagnose a 'civic crisis'.[1] Two years later, turnout for elections for the new Scottish Parliament, seen by constitutional reformers as a catalyst for democratic renewal, fell below 50 per cent.

Yet outside the conventional political arena, civic life in Britain has been far from inert. In September 2000 groups of fuel price protesters, equipped with mobile phones and taking their cue from farmers in France, blockaded oil refineries and created a national emergency, catching the government unawares. The Countryside

Alliance brought 400,000 people onto the streets of London in September 2002. Five months later, there were a million demonstrators against the imminent war in Iraq.

In Scotland, the new parliament was expected to spend its first year tackling student tuition fees and land reform. What erupted instead was a volcanic row over whether the new coalition government should repeal Section 28, a law forbidding the 'promotion' of homosexuality in schools. More than 1.2 million people – in a population of five million – voted against repeal in an unofficial referendum funded by a businessman and championed by the *Daily Record*, Scotland's biggest-selling daily newspaper.

The American journalist Walter Lippmann called the making of public opinion 'the manufacture of consent'.[2] A lifetime later, the process continues but the product has changed: from consent to dissent.

Street protests in themselves are nothing new, nor have modern communications transformed them out of all recognition. It is possible to imagine the Chartists texting one another as they massed on Kennington Common to lobby Parliament in 1848. Equally, newspapers have a history of mobilising opinion, from duelling over Dreyfus in 1890s Paris to balloting black readers for their choice of mayor in 1950s Chicago. What is new is the congruence of direct action, a partisan press in search of causes, and an electorate dissatisfied with the party system.

I want to suggest that newspapers, faced with falling circulation and competition from the internet, are joining the twenty-first century version of the picket line. This press activism has helped foster a new kind of social movement: dramatic surges of single-issue sentiment that occur outside party politics and which can be activated by surprisingly small groups of people. Noam Chomsky, borrowing from Lippmann, charged the media with 'manufacturing consent' to serve the interests of the powerful.[3] But Lippmann described a more complex interaction between public opinion and the press, and my argument follows his.

As used here, the phrase 'manufacturing dissent' implies not a media conspiracy but a synthesis between protest movements, press campaigns, and public opinion that takes place outside the party system. Protesters want instant attention from government; newspapers want instant attention from readers. No single player controls the manufacturing process, and the product depends on more than a headline-writer's wit or editor's whim.

Indeed, none of the recent protests succeeded in their primary aims. Gordon Brown did not slash the price of ordinary petrol, although he did make concessions on diesel and cleaner fuel. Labour banned foxhunting, although it took seven years to do so. The Scottish Executive repealed Section 28, with the rest of the UK following three years later. Tony Blair committed British armed forces to fight alongside US troops in the war against Iraq.

Perhaps as a result, these 'flash moments' – the phrase belongs to the Harvard professor Joseph Nye[4] – have been under-analysed and often dismissed, unlike the anti-globalisation movement, which has received wide and often enthusiastic attention.[5]

Direct action tends to be bracketed with the left. But the fuel protesters, Section 28 campaigners and Countryside Alliance championed causes more usually associated with the right: lower taxes, moral values and the defence of rural life. In each case the protest blew up abruptly, startling politicians with its intensity. In each case there was vigorous newspaper backing, often sliding from editorial endorsement into outright instigation. In each case the storm subsided quickly, leaving the political class to breathe a sigh of relief and get on with the business of elected government.

These flash moments deserve attention for reasons both disturbing and encouraging. On the one hand, they suggest that public frustration will find an outlet and is easily manipulated; on the other, that British democracy is far from moribund. But they are not being taken as seriously as they deserve. Beyond a desire to harness the vitality and technological savvy of social movements – as Howard Dean's campaign for the Democratic nomination tried to do – politicians have little incentive to think through the implications for twenty-first century politics.

For this symbiosis between press and protest implies both a critique of political parties and a challenge to them. The fuel blockades were a threat to representative democracy, as ministers were quick to point out. Media tactics such as the privately funded Section 28 referendum also challenge the legitimacy of electoral politics by mimicking the electoral process.

The press, too, stays largely silent about its role in mobilising public opinion. The convention in British journalism is not to mention other newspapers unless to attack them. Yet newspapers were clearly players in the fuel protests, the defence of hunting and the Section 28 campaign. The *Sun*, the *Mail* and the *Record* are in the Leninist vanguard of contemporary protest.

However evanescent these movements may have been, they hold clues to what our democracy might look like in 2050. The single-issue, press-backed campaign implies a shift to a consumer-driven politics that demands immediate response. The lack of fit between party platforms and protesters' concerns suggests a dissonance between politics and public opinion. The axis with media organisations creates powerful if short-lived coalitions capable of competing with governments to frame the political agenda.

The trend towards instant, PR-driven protest risks giving newspapers disproportionate power. It pushes politicians into the role of rapid reactors to majority pressure, rather than arbiters of different interests. But it is a logical, not irrational, response to the growing irrelevance and insularity of the party system.

2. Protest: from footprint to newsprint

Guests arriving at Chequers for the 50th birthday of the Prime Minister's wife were held up by pro-hunting protesters, including a naked man in a Tony Blair mask. The host opted to defuse the situation by inviting some of the gatecrashers in for a chat.

This was not the first time that the Prime Minister's plans had been derailed by protest. In September 2000, Mr Blair arrived in Hull to celebrate John Prescott's 30 years in Parliament, only to find the town hall surrounded blocked by fuel price demonstrators. A few years later, an activist from Fathers 4 Justice threw purple flour at him in the House of Commons. Mr Prescott himself was involved in a scuffle with a farm worker during the 2001 election campaign.

While most party leaders expect to duck the occasional rotten tomato, Labour's years in office have been haunted by spasmodic outbreaks of public anger. From the Countryside Alliance marches to the fuel protests, from the Section 28 row in Scotland to the demonstrations before the bombing of Iraq, these spectacular shows of instant protest have taken politicians by surprise. Raids on field trials of GM crops inspired a plot line in *The Archers* – a sure sign that direct action techniques had become an accepted part of British life.

In itself, extra-parliamentary action is familiar. The anti-war marchers recalled their predecessors in the 1950s and the 1980s. The fuel price protesters, while unusually effective in bringing the country to a halt, fit into a long tradition of anti-tax revolts, most recently against the poll tax. Some of their tactics of converging, blockading and text-messaging were learnt from environmentalists opposing new road schemes and rave party organisers challenging public order laws.

So why pay any more attention to a demonstration now than a demonstration ten years ago? Three reasons. Conventional party politics is slowly dying. The protest agenda has extended beyond the familiar left and green issues. And newspapers, threatened by declining circulation and the interactive internet, are co-opting protest movements in pursuit of favourite causes.

The slow death of party politics

Across the European Union, people are turning away from politics and political parties, as turnout falls and partisan loyalties wither. At the present rate of decline, the three main parties in Britain will have no members left in ten years' time.

When Labour came to power in 1997, some held up constitutional change as the way to revitalise a tired democracy. While Tony Blair resisted voting reform, he set up a Scottish Parliament and a Welsh Assembly, both elected under a more proportional system than the House of Commons. But devolution has not proved the democratic tonic that campaigners expected. Turnout dropped by nearly ten points between the first and second set of elections to the Scottish Parliament; in Wales, it dropped eight points to 38 per cent. When the North East of England was offered an elected assembly only 48 per cent of the regional electorate voted, with 78 per cent of them rejecting the idea.

Far from becoming the fulcrum of Scottish public life, the Parliament was not the crucible for the Section 28 controversy which occupied much of its first year. The row, over the repeal of a law which forbade the 'promotion' of homosexuality, was fought out mainly in the media. The new voting system has allowed voters in Scotland a chance to elect candidates from outside the main parties. The 2003 Holyrood elections yielded a 'rainbow' result, including seven Greens, six Scottish Socialists, a 74-year-old from a pensioners' party and a GP campaigning against hospital closures. The surprise success of Dr Jean Turner, who defeated a Labour MSP in Strathkelvin and Bearsden, mirrored that of Dr Richard Taylor, who won a seat from Labour in the 2001 general election by opposing the run-down of a local hospital.

While a handful of results do not make a trend, they alerted nervous ministers to the voter volatility that was already evident in other EU countries. In the Netherlands, Pim Fortuyn's new anti-immigration party entered government on a wave of popular support after his assassination in 2002. Britain experienced its own upheaval in the European elections of 2004, when the UK Independence Party, energised by the arrival of television presenter Robert Kilroy-Silk, won 12 seats on a platform of withdrawal from the European Union.

In response, Labour politicians warned that disaffected voters could be targeted by the far right, a fear apparently confirmed by the BNP's plan to field a record number of candidates in the 2005 general election. But for Douglas Alexander, a UK minister representing a Scottish constituency, the Holyrood results suggested another trend: a shift away from orthodox parties towards 'the passing whims of populism'. While others were celebrating the diversity of the new rainbow Parliament, he warned that voting for single-issue candidates was not a 'risk-free life-style statement', and could lead to irresponsible government.[6]

The rise of protest

While people are opting not to vote or choosing alternative candidates, other forms of political action are on the rise. Research shows that the percentage prepared to go on a protest demonstration has risen from 20 per cent in 1979 to 33 per cent in 2000.[7] This seems to be a Europe-wide trend. A study of 12 European countries between 1974 and 1990 found a rise in grassroots activity in every country except Spain.[8] There are fashions in protest, as in politics. While the British are less likely to attend a public meeting or sign a petition than they were 15 years ago, they are more likely to contact the media or get involved in a consumer boycott.[9]

Tempting as it is to jump to the conclusion that this indicates the emergence of an alternative or 'new politics', the evidence does not suggest so. Researchers have searched in vain for proof that people who do not vote are more likely to take part in protest activities – with the important exception of the young who are less likely to vote in any case. If anything, protesters are good democrats; they just have an extra trick up their sleeve. One survey found that 87 per cent of those who had ever been on a demonstration had also voted in the 1997 general election, compared with 71 per cent of those who had never taken to the streets.[10] A study of people demonstrating in Glasgow against imminent war with Iraq found that 80 per cent had voted in the 2001 general election, far higher than the actual turnout.[11]

From replacing conventional politics, protest has become an accepted part of the political repertoire, such that it is now considered normal for elderly women to picket the export of veal calves or for the Tory party leader to join the Countryside Alliance march. According to the American political scientist Russell Dalton, this is common to most advanced industrial societies. 'Protest is now predominantly seen as an expansion of the democratic process to citizen-orientated, elite-challenging activities rather than as opposition to democracy.'[12]

The question is, if people who protest are not abandoning the ballot box, why are they taking to the streets or 'swarming' on the internet? One possible answer is that political parties are not spotting 'hot' issues, not responding quickly enough, or simply ignoring them.

Even though polls showed widespread mistrust of genetically modified crops, the government was slow to acknowledge public concern, belatedly announcing a 'public debate' before giving the go-ahead for the commercial growing of GM maize.

In the case of Section 28, the backlash against repeal took ministers in Scotland by surprise. While the Scottish Conservatives were opposed, the loudest objections came from the Catholic Church, and the campaign did not gather steam until a wealthy businessman and a tabloid newspaper became involved.

As for the fuel protests, the Prime Minister's strategist and pollster, Philip Gould, had warned for months that voters were unhappy about the price of petrol, prompting Gordon Brown to scrap the fuel price escalator (brought in by the Tories) in his March 2000 Budget.[13] So ministers were aware of the issue but failed to foresee that protests by farmers and hauliers in France would spread across the Channel with such dramatic effect.

If protest indicates frustration, it also shows impatience. Could it be that, in a media age that values instant gratification and high-octane outbursts, voting seems too bloodless a way for voters to express their views? Why wait five years to vent your spleen when, with the aid of a mobile phone, you can fix a protest in five hours? Just as parties are too slow off the mark, the electoral cycle is too sedate to accommodate surges of anger and single-issue fixations. A generation that can vote someone out of the *Big Brother* house in a matter of minutes will be disinclined to queue patiently for the ballot box.

The changing face of protest

Direct action is not only becoming more common: it is being re-claimed across the political spectrum. Twentieth-century protest has been associated with the left, from the Jarrow March and the peace movement to the student sit-ins of the 1960s and trade-union disputes of the 1970s, culminating in the anti-capitalist showings at summits in Seattle and Genoa.

But stunts and blockades, pickets and demos are not inherently left-wing tactics. They can be used by anyone, to further any cause – like the anti-Catholic Gordon riots in the 1780s, or the fascist marches of the 1930s. During the fuel crisis John Monks, former TUC general secretary, invoked a right-wing tradition of protest by recalling another occasion 'when trucks and lorries were used by the self-employed and the far right to attack democracy'. He meant the 1973 coup in Chile which brought down Salvador Allende.

With the decline of organised labour, protest is no longer a left-wing preserve. It has been reclaimed by anyone who feels their identity to be threatened, be they polo players resisting a ban on fox-hunting, fishermen's wives angry at North Sea quotas, or parents anxious about sex education in schools. The French sociologist Alain Touraine describes these rearguard actions as 'anti-movements'.[14]

Monks's reference to a socialist martyr highlighted the hypocrisy in attitudes to protest. Your view of the cause dictates your view of the methods. When five pro-hunt protesters got into the Commons chamber in September 2004, the anti-hunt *Guardian* called them 'thugs' and their protest 'a desecration of the basic principles of democracy and law'. For the pro-hunt *Daily Mail*, they were 'otherwise honest people feeling pushed into civil disobedience'.[15]

Media protest

Protest has always relied on symbolism. When the suffragettes stormed the gates of Buckingham Palace, it made as good a picture as when Batman and Robin from Fathers 4 Justice scaled the royal walls in September 2004. But the dominance of television has turned protest into performance art, short-lived tableaux that need not have a swell of numbers behind them. Emmeline Pankhurst had 20,000 suffragettes with her when she tried to see the king in May 1914. Jason Hatch, dressed as Batman, had only one companion, dressed as Robin – and got the grievances of divorced fathers onto every front page.

Where once you needed a shop steward to organise a demonstration, now you need him to call the picture desks or post on a weblog. One powerful image can trump strength in numbers. As the French social theorist Pierre Bourdieu reflected, 'Television can produce an effect close to what you'd have from 50,000 in the streets.'[16] José Bové, the French farmer and activist, led a mere 500 farmers to storm a branch of McDonald's in south-west France, in a protest against US trade restrictions on foods such as *foie gras* and Roquefort cheese.

While the familiar kinds of protest persist (in the demonstrations against war with Iraq, for example), we are also seeing the emergence of virtual protest: enacted through images, articulated through the media. The aftermath of Diana's death, that strange blend of royal icons, grieving crowds and vanilla republicanism, may have speeded the process.

Countryside Alliance campaigners have, from the start, been able to count on powerful press allies, especially at the *Daily Telegraph* and the *Daily Mail*, to give them a voice and keep the issue alive even as the government tried to let it die. The *Telegraph* organised a debate at the annual Game Fair on 'Protest and breaking the law'. Charles Moore, the former editor, had a poster in his office and went on Countryside Alliance demonstrations. Around the same time Rosie Boycott, then editor of the *Independent on Sunday*, was to be found addressing a London rally for the decriminalisation of cannabis.

There have always been editors with hobby horses and proprietors with a cause. Lords Beaverbrook and Rothermere, owners of the *Daily Express* and the *Daily Mail*, founded their own party to field free-trade candidates against Stanley Baldwin's Conservatives. Rothermere later lent his papers' backing to Oswald Mosley's British Union of Fascists, producing the headlines 'Hurrah for the Blackshirts' and 'Lend the Blackshirts a helping hand' in the *Mail* and the *Mirror*.[17]

But press-protest means more than backing a cause. It involves the creation of a self-referential universe where politicians have at best a walk-on part, and where small groups can have their voices hugely amplified. Sir Andrew Green, a retired diplomat who runs Migration Watch, has been quoted at least once a week on the issue of asylum in the *Daily Express* and the *Daily Star* since the start of 2003.

The Section 28 debate took the manufacture of dissent to a new level, being fought almost entirely by and through the media. There were demonstrations, but they came mainly from supporters of repeal, such as gay groups, students and trade unionists. The Keep the Clause campaign made its case with billboards, paid for by the businessman Brian Souter, and a flow of stories in the *Daily Record*, the *Daily Mail* and the *Sun*. Rather than a campaign in the conventional sense, there were a couple of names, principally Jack Irvine, Mr Souter's public relations adviser, whom reporters routinely rang for quotes. (One of Mr Irvine's subsequent clients was the Countryside Alliance in Scotland.)

The question is, when does the press cross the line between covering protest and sponsoring it? And how does that influence the democratic process? For the Section 28 affair was by no means wholly virtual. It culminated in hard numbers, as the *Daily Record* mimicked politics with a referendum on whether the law should be kept or scrapped. More than a million Scots voted, of whom 87 per cent favoured retention. Yet the Executive went ahead with repeal.

Three years later the *Daily Mail* ran its own UK-wide ballot on whether the new EU constitution should be put a referendum of the British people rather than simply approved by MPs. On this occasion 1.7 million people voted, of whom 89 per cent were in favour. The following April, Tony Blair announced that the government would indeed hold a referendum – prompting the *Sun*, which had been running a campaign of its own, to tell readers, 'EU did it!'

It is not just that protest is migrating from the streets into the pages of newspapers. With the shift from footprint to newsprint has come another change. Instead of reporting dissent, the media is shaping and making it.

3. Case studies: the press on the picket line

If the charge is incitement, the case is hard to make. Media responsibility is not just controversial but difficult to prove. How do you distinguish between reporting protest and fomenting it? Between reflecting and manufacturing dissent?

Under a first-past-the-post voting system, the press plays a useful role in highlighting issues that a government with a parliamentary majority is free to overlook. Indeed, newspapers often make the claim that they are the real agents of democracy, giving voice to the 'silent majority' whose views on a given issue are ignored by the governing elite.

The day after the pro-hunting raid on the Commons in September 2004, Peter Oborne hailed this 'silent majority' in the *Daily Mail*. Bracketing together the issues of hunting, fuel prices and EU integration, he condemned Labour as a government that 'does not listen'.[18] But the 'silent majority' is often invoked rhetorically. While feelings run high over foxhunting, for example, polls clearly show a majority favouring a ban or some form of regulation.

On issues such as Section 28, the picture is less clear. Supporters of repeal say that the controversy was stirred up by newspapers, in particular the *Daily Record*, which spearheaded the campaign against repeal. The *Daily Record* would retort that it was simply reflecting public opinion – the 'silent majority' for whom, as the paper claimed in an editorial, repeal was far from a priority. Polls did indeed suggest a majority in favour of keeping the clause, but these were carried out after it had already become a *cause célèbre*. We do not have before-and-after surveys that could help assess the effect of press coverage on public opinion.

Experts struggle to isolate the 'media effect'. They puzzle over whether newspapers are mouthpieces which merely articulate protest, or 'primary definers' which create it. Stefaan Walgrave, a political scientist from Antwerp, tried to test this distinction with a study of the White March, the biggest demonstration in Belgian history.[19] In 1996, after the murder of four little girls by the paedophile Marc Dutroux, 300,000 people took to the streets of Brussels for a silent demonstration, carrying white balloons and flowers. Where usually political parties and trade unions would have organised the event, on this occasion newspapers acted as recruiting sergeants. Saturation coverage beforehand, including diaries by the victims' parents, was accompanied by practical tips on where to park and how to get cheap train tickets. 'See you in Brussels on Sunday', read one headline.

According to Walgrave, 'the media made the White March'. A second march a year later was much less successful, he suggests – only 30,000 people turned out – because newspaper attention had faded. Walgrave concludes that the press can only mobilise protest under certain conditions. The cause needs to be simple and non-political; people must trust the media; and the media should not be too ideologically polarised. Yet the UK has a partisan media and the lowest level of trust in pre-enlargement Europe.[20]

Three case studies may shed light on whether British newspapers should be charged with incitement or praised for responsive journalism. All occurred during 2000, a year that was remarkable for political passions outside party politics.[21]

Paedophiles, Paulsgrove and the *News of the World*
Background
The murder in July 2000 of eight-year-old Sarah Payne led to an extraordinary series of events in which the UK's biggest-selling tabloid newspaper provoked a riot and changed government policy.

Long before Sarah's naked body was found, the press was assuming that a paedophile was responsible. The *News of the World*, a Sunday tabloid from the Murdoch-owned News International stable, pledged 'to expose these monsters and to see that they are locked away'.[22]

On 23 July, the Sunday after the body was found, the *News of the World* began publishing the names of convicted paedophiles, under the headline 'Does a monster live near you?' It argued that parents had a right to know in order to protect their children. With the blessing of Sarah's parents, the paper called for 'Sarah's Law', allowing public access to the confidential register of paedophiles – an idea modelled on 'Megan's Law' in the US.

This was not the first time a newspaper had 'outed' convicted paedophiles. The *Daily Record* published 38 names in 1997, while regional papers in the UK and Italy had done the same.

Manufacturing dissent?

Although the *News of the World* insisted that its campaign was 'absolutely NOT a charter for vigilantes', vigilante action followed. A man in Manchester found his house surrounded by neighbours who mistook him for a paedophile. A family in Plymouth had to leave their home. In Gwent a doctor found graffiti on her walls after someone confused 'paedophile' with 'paediatrician'.

Despite pleas from the Home Secretary, children's charities, police and probation, the *News of the World* continued with a second week of 'naming and shaming'. Experts warned that it could drive paedophiles into hiding. The paper retorted that the high reoffending rate among paedophiles showed the system was not working.[23]

Among the second tranche of named men was Victor Burnett, who lived on the Paulsgrove estate near Portsmouth. On 3 August, a crowd attacked his house with bottles and stones, injuring a policeman and overturning a car. Children held placards saying 'Pervs should burn'.

The reaction from other papers was disapproving, with the exception of the *Daily Mirror*, which supported 'Sarah's Law'. The *Independent* and the *Daily Telegraph*, usually at odds on law and order issues, united in condemning the *News of the World*'s campaign. The

Sun, its sister paper, held aloof. Other national and regional newspapers routinely used the word 'mob' to describe protests in Paulsgrove and elsewhere.

The Paynes, about to bury their daughter, were appalled. 'We never wanted this. We don't want any violence, and we can't bear to see children like this, brought up to hate,' said Sarah's mother.[24]

On 6 August the *News of the World* announced it would suspend publication of more names, explaining that the police, the probation service and the NSPCC had agreed to work on 'Sarah's Charter', a blueprint for reform. Notwithstanding a 700,000 petition presented by Sarah's parents, the government refused to allow public access to the sex offenders' register. But ministers agreed to tighten up the law in other ways, with stricter controls on newly released paedophiles and advance warning for their victims.

Rioting went on for a week in Paulsgrove, until residents agreed to give police their list of suspected paedophiles. Council officers offered to re-house those on the list who felt threatened. While some of those named had convictions for sex offences – though not against children – none were thought to be a risk to the community. Thirty-six of the rioters, many of them juveniles, were later charged with public order offences.

Outcomes

The *News of the World*'s campaign was revived briefly 18 months later, after Roy Whiting, who had been released from prison after serving four years for abducting and indecently assaulting a nine-year-old girl, was convicted of Sarah's murder. The paper published photographs, supplied by Scotland Yard, of four paedophiles who had gone to ground – an action praised by John Prescott, Deputy Prime Minister, as 'public spirited'.

David Blunkett, who had succeeded Jack Straw as Home Secretary, met the Paynes after the trial and assured them that 'seven-eighths of Sarah's law has been implemented'. This included provision for longer sentences and stricter supervision but not, crucially, public access to the register.

Professor Chas Critcher, author of *Moral Panics and the Media*, suggests that the newspaper was less powerful an agent than it seemed. Ministers, he points out, were already reviewing the law on sexual offences. 'The NOW campaign was an immediate nuisance to government but in the long run helped create conditions conducive to extraordinary measures that the government was already contemplating.'[25]

The *News of the World* could legitimately claim that public opinion was behind it. Rebekah Wade commissioned a MORI poll – from a relatively small sample of 614 – which found that 88 per cent backed the principle of Sarah's law. Other papers agreed that the government was out of touch with the strength of feeling on the issue. 'Politicians can be in no doubt that alarm about known child abusers being placed on estates is widespread and potentially explosive,' editorialised the *Daily Mail*. 'Lynch law only flourishes when public policy and public opinion are radically out of balance.'[26]

Alongside the debate about whether the *News of the World* was right, a discussion began – among police, lawyers, psychologists and probation officers – about the monitoring and treatment of paedophiles. But neither the populist clamour nor the professional dialogue involved party politics. There was consensus on the need for longer sentences and more rigorous tracking of paedophiles. The Conservatives made no political capital from the campaign for Sarah's law. William Hague, then Tory leader, commented that 'resort to the rule of the mob is absolutely wrong', and supported the Home Secretary in resisting public access to the register. The *News of the World* attacked Mr Hague for 'sitting on the fence'.[27]

For Paulsgrove, the episode brought both notoriety and results. A few months after the riots, it received a Home Office grant for local estate patrols. The local Labour MP, Syd Rapson, later reflected that while he deplored the violence and involvement of children, the authorities were now aware of what would happen if they 'dumped' paedophiles on the estate. 'It was a sad process but a lot of good has come out of it, including extra investment in Paulsgrove,' he said.[28]

Katrina Kessell, one of the ringleaders, believed that Paulsgrove had become 'the safest estate in England'. She was pleased that the protesters – predominantly working-class, including a high proportion of single mothers – had made their voice heard.[29]

Sarah Payne's parents were also given a voice by the campaign, moving from the role of grieving parents to lobbyists for criminal justice reform. Her mother remarked that without the *News of the World*, they would never have been invited to sit around the same table as the Home Secretary.[30]

The effects on the paper were mixed. It added 95,000 copies on the first Sunday of the 'naming and shaming', but the campaign had no long-term effect on sales, which remained around the four million mark. Rebekah Wade was criticised for declining to go on television to justify her editorial stance. (She did appear on *Breakfast with Frost* in December 2001, before accompanying the Paynes to a meeting with David Blunkett.) Two and a half years after Paulsgrove she moved to the *Sun*, hailed by Rupert Murdoch as 'a great campaigning editor'.

The chairman of the home affairs select committee called for Ms Wade to be prosecuted for incitement to public order offences, but no action was taken. Her critics argued that using words like 'monsters' and 'beasts' was bound to stir up hatred, and that the paper undermined confidence in official tracking of released paedophiles, prompting people to take the law into their own hands. The *News of the World*'s defence was that it had warned repeatedly against vigilantism, and that the system was not working. It would also be fair to point out that 'naming and shaming' has been used by other newspapers – to drive kerbcrawlers out of a neighbourhood, for example – without leading to violence.

The nearest the *News of the World* came to an official rebuke was in a different context. After the double murder of Holly Wells and Jessica Chapman in 2003, it was one of several newspapers investigated by the Attorney General for possible contempt of court. The paper had urged readers to cut out coupons calling for the introduction of Sarah's law, publishing them alongside pictures of Holly and Jessica. This implied – or so his lawyer argued at his trial – that Huntley was a paedophile, which could have prejudiced a jury.

No action was taken against the *News of the World*, although the Attorney General became more active in issuing contempt warnings. The episode illustrates the narrow frame of reference for media accountability. If a newspaper is suspected of skewing someone's trial, there are mechanisms to hold it responsible; but what if it is accused of starting a riot?

I find it quite astonishing that an editor can launch a campaign and cause such predictable problems and then attempt to maintain a Trappist silence about her role in it.

Robin Corbett, Home Affairs Select Committee Chairman,
21 Aug 2000

Freedom and the price of petrol

Background

For a week in September 2000, Britain was in crisis. Cars queued at those petrol stations that remained open. There was panic-buying at supermarkets as ad hoc groups of farmers and truckers blockaded oil refineries across the country. The Prime Minister pleaded with oil executives to get deliveries out. As one minister recalled, 'We were twenty-four hours from meltdown, at best 48 hours away.'[31]

The precipitating cause was the rise in crude oil prices to a ten-year high of $35 a barrel, mainly due to instability in the Middle East. The surge was especially noticeable in the UK, aggravated by the twin effect of high fuel duty and VAT.

Britain, however, was far from alone in experiencing unrest. There were fuel price protests across Europe, in France, Germany, Ireland, Italy, the Netherlands, Sweden and Hungary. For many countries, that week in September was the culmination of campaigns by farmers and hauliers who were struggling with low profit margins.

In Britain, their tactics came as a surprise. Dissatisfied with their conventional lobby organisations, the National Farmers' Union and the Road Hauliers' Association, breakaway groups like Farmers for Action had began to use direct action techniques learnt from road protesters and environmentalists. In March 1999, for example, more than a year before the fuel protests, 1,000 truckers had blocked London's Park Lane in protest at diesel duty and the road tax on lorries.[32]

At the same time, consumer pressure was being expressed through organisations like the AA and the RAC. The controversy in Scotland over road tolls – an idea proposed by the Executive and then dropped – created a perception in the press that ministers were persecuting motorists. The government was aware of this and Gordon Brown had scrapped the 'fuel duty escalator' in his Budget of March 2000.[33]

Ministers were already dealing with a backlash against Labour's commitment to ban foxhunting, which had become identified with the defence of rural life. Since motorists in remote areas had particular reason to resent the price of fuel, the two causes overlapped. Margaret Beckett, a Cabinet minister, referred to the fuel protesters as 'the industrial wing of the Countryside Alliance'.[34]

Manufacturing dissent?

The *Daily Mail's* campaign kicked off with the May Bank Holiday ('highest price yet for the gallon as Bank Holiday rush starts'). Throughout June and July, the paper ran stories highlighting the high cost of petrol. There were comparisons with other EU countries and reports that drivers were paying more in fuel and road tax than in income tax. The *Mail* also blamed petrol prices for driving nurses out of the NHS and causing a 'forecourt crimewave' as motorists fled the pumps without paying.

Not to be outdone, the paper's Scottish edition reported that tourists were being kept away by the high cost of petrol, and featured a coach driver who brought diesel from Germany to save money on a Highland tour. But it was not until 29 June that the *Mail* went full throttle, with a front page headline 'Petrol prices: the great revolt'.

This turned out to be free publicity for a 'Dump the Pump' boycott, planned for 1 August and coordinated by two salesmen from Berkshire. The *Mail* predicted 'an explosion of public anger'.

The headline the following day was 'Petrol – the Revolt grows', based on a surge of calls to the paper and hits on the boycotters' website. The story continued: 'The *Daily Mail*'s campaign for a cut in petrol duty triggered an unprecedented display of grassroots anger. Motorists through the country, from industry chiefs to self-employed tradesmen, from families with children at school to pensioners, insisted the highway robbery has to stop.' Interviews with people from different walks of life created the impression of a broad coalition of support.

The campaign was targeted personally at the Chancellor. 'People paying the price of Gordon's greed,' was the title of one story exploring how petrol prices were affecting everyday life. The *Mail* gave away car stickers depicting Mr Brown as a highway robber. The *Sun* was running a parallel campaign of its own – 'Get it down, Brown' – with a 300,000-strong petition for the Chancellor. The two papers showed signs of shadowing one another, with the *Sun* also featuring references to 'Gordon's greed' and 'Brown the highwayman'. No other papers were so single-minded or so *ad hominem* in pursuit of cheaper petrol.

The singling out of the Chancellor was not inevitable. The campaign could have been targeted at the Prime Minister. It could have called for cheaper alternatives to petrol. It could have blamed the oil companies for not passing on price cuts to the consumer. It could have blamed OPEC, which was engaged in a squabble about whether to increase oil production, with Venezuela leading the resistance.

Yet in an editorial at the height of the crisis, the *Mail* took care to clear OPEC of blame: 'The crisis at the British pumps hasn't been caused by the sheikhs but by New Labour's stealth taxes.'[35] The price of petrol was attributed solely to the government's desire to raise revenue. Until the protests began, the only significant criticism of the oil companies was when BP paid £132 million for a new logo.[36]

What actually happened on 1 August, the day of the 'Dump the Pump' boycott, was variously portrayed. The *Mail* ran an editorial the previous day entitled 'Anger Mr Brown cannot ignore,' effectively committing itself to a decent turnout. On 2 August it reported 'Up to a million motorists backed a massive protest against Gordon Brown's sky high fuel taxes.' The *Sun* put the figure at 9 million.

The Press Association, by contrast, found only 'a small drop in custom'. Regional papers agreed, with the *Coventry Evening Telegraph* reporting 'business as usual' and the *South Wales Evening Post* finding, 'Pump campaign dumped by drivers'. A planned truckers' protest 'fell flat', according to PA, when only 12 turned up out of an expected 200.

This episode suggests that newspapers cannot, of themselves, foment protest. The fuel blockades did not begin until 9 September, by which time the *Mail* and the *Sun* had been campaigning hard on the issue for at least two months. The precipitating factor seems to have been the success of protests by French farmers, fishermen and truckers. After a week of blockades which brought emergency petrol rationing, they won a series of concessions from Lionel Jospin's Socialist government, including rebates for truckers, a cut in fuel tax and a one-off windfall tax on oil company profits.

While some of the French activists were known to their UK counterparts, Brian Doherty of Keele University concludes that the media were the crucial transmission channel. 'It seems most likely that it was images from France, relayed through the media, rather than personal contact, that explained the spread of the fuel protests to Britain.'[37]

The print press was at first hostile, combining xenophobia with concern for British tourists caught up in a farmers' blockade of the Channel Tunnel. The *Mail* criticised French 'bullyboys', while the *Sun* deplored the 'holiday mayhem'.

On 7 September, truckers and farmers voted to blockade the oil refinery at Stanlow in Ellesmere Port, Cheshire, prompting the *Mail's* front-page: 'British farmers copycat blockade'. In a leader, 'Afflicted by the French epidemic', the paper contrasted 'bloody-minded militancy' with the opportunity for 'peaceful and legal dissent' in a 'grown-up parliamentary democracy'.

In the days which followed, the *Mail* continued to condemn the protesters' tactics, while engaging in a war of words with the government over the reason for high fuel prices. Ministers insisted that a 2p cut on a litre of petrol would mean slashing public spending by £1 billion, a statistic condemned by the paper as 'the great tax lie'.

While decrying 'the civil disobedience convulsing this country', the *Mail* also carried friendly features describing 'a very British blockade', in which pickets made cups of tea and tuned in to Radio 4. By contrast, the Chancellor was described as 'smirking' and the government as 'cynical, arrogant and out of touch'.[38]

The *Sun* was similarly ambivalent. While condemning the protesters as 'secondary pickets' (and warning that pubs could run out of beer), the paper playfully compared this 'people's uprising' to other 'all-time British revolts', including the Tolpuddle Martyers, the Peasants' Revolt and the poll tax riots – the last of which, needless to say, it did not support at the time. Yet the day after celebrating 'a very British blockade', the *Mail* was calling on the protesters to give up. 'You have fought honourably, made your point with stunning success and despite causing disruption to millions achieved an astonishingly high level of support.'[39]

The *Sun* was also confused, attacking Tony Blair for 'not listening' to public anger over fuel prices, then commending him for 'showing leadership' in facing down the pickets. The following day it continued to equivocate about the Prime Minister's position while being more definite about the protesters. 'We do not condone this action. We prefer the democratic way.'[40]

As the protesters called 'a dignified halt', the *Mail* hailed them for 'still commanding the moral high ground', dismissing suggestions that oil-tanker drivers had been intimidated. (The following month, police and trade unions produced separate dossiers cataloguing threats, abuse and assault, described by the Home Secretary as 'intolerable'.)

Part of the protesters' case for calling off their action was to wait for Gordon Brown's pre-Budget report, due in November. Attempts to revive the protests nearer that time met with short shrift. 'It is as friends that we urge the protesters to think long and hard before taking further action, even if they are disappointed by Gordon Brown's PBR later this month,' editorialised the *Mail*. 'Most people will not back the protests if real hardship results,' warned the *Sun*.[41]

The government publicised its readiness to use the police and the army to break further blockades. The Chancellor, while not cutting fuel duty as the protesters demanded, unveiled a package that made 'green' fuel cheaper, lowered road tax for lorries and scrapped it altogether for tractors. The *Mail* felt that Mr Brown 'shows it pays to protest', and the *Sun* agreed he had 'taken the heat' out of the demonstrations.[42] An attempt at reviving them with a convoy of trucks converging on London fizzled out with a few hundred drivers.

Outcomes

The protests gave the government a major fright. Tony Blair was particularly shaken by his inability to get results from meeting oil company executives – although this did not stop Anji Hunter, his personal private secretary, from taking a job with BP a year later. Ironically, given Mr Blair's efforts to distance Labour from the trade unions, it was the Transport and General Workers' Union which came to the rescue by persuading tanker drivers to leave the depots.

Phone-in polls during the protests showed public opinion was with the protesters and against the government, a trend confirmed when, for the first and only time since Labour came to power in 1997, the Conservatives moved ahead in the opinion polls. The collapse in support for Labour was concentrated among working-class voters – which, since they are less likely to own cars, suggests that this was more than a motorists' revolt.[43] For the Tories, however, the effect was short-lived. Their poll lead was lost within a month. William Hague went into the 2001 election promising to cut petrol by 6p a litre, with no obvious electoral benefit.

The longer-term effect was to stymie any discussion of how to limit car use or use fuel taxes to curb climate change. Green arguments were barely heard during the fuel protests, which were framed entirely as an argument about tax, with ministers arguing that the extra revenue was needed for public services and the health of the economy. The same newspapers which backed petrol price cuts featured stories about climate change and looming environmental catastrophe.[44]

While the protesters did not get the cut in duty which they sought, they made it politically difficult for duty to be raised. Just how difficult became clear in the summer of 2004, when violence in Iraq and terrorist attacks in Saudi Arabia pushed oil prices up to $39 a barrel, and petrol to 85p a litre.

The Chancellor, having frozen fuel duty since 2000, was planning to increase it by 2p a litre in the autumn. But as discontented murmurings grew, David Handley from Farmers for Action forecast a series of protests in cities across the country. Days before they were due to go ahead, the Chancellor said he would review his decision, citing 'the worries of motorists, hauliers and business generally'.[45] Apart from a couple of convoys in Scotland and Wales, his announcement – together with an OPEC production increase and a supermarket price-cutting war – was sufficient to defuse the threat.

But an implicit ban on raising revenue from fuel leaves the Chancellor constrained. If he is to cut car emissions and tackle congestion, his only options are to raise vehicle excise duty or consider road pricing, which the *Mail* and the *Sun* hotly opposed when the Scottish Executive tried to introduce it north of the Border. Yet on the same day as Mr Brown's decision was formally announced, Alistair Darling, the transport secretary, unveiled a white paper that included plans for road pricing.[46] By leaping to the aid of the motorist, the *Sun* and the *Mail* may have hastened the arrival of a more radical policy.

How much responsibility for the protests can be laid at their door? Farmers and hauliers had been staging blockades long before the summer of 2000. The *Mail*'s publicity for 'Dump the Pump' had minimal effect. A few days of TV images from France probably had more practical impact than weeks of highly coloured headlines.

Even at the height of the fuel crisis, the *Sun* was quick to ward off accusations of incitement. 'The petrol protests were spontaneous,' it insisted. 'They were not planned – and they have not been whipped up by media support.'[47] But Professor Brian Doherty of Keele University concludes that the dominant effect of the media 'was to create legitimacy for the protests and their cause'.[48]

The former *Daily Mirror* editor Roy Greenslade, writing when the crisis had passed, was especially critical of 'cosy interviews' with picket leaders. He felt they were cast as 'hard-done-by heroes', and contrasted their treatment with the scrutiny that striking trade unionists would have received from papers like the *Mail* and the *Sun*.[49] (The *Mail* was to be highly critical of union leaders during the 2002 firefighters' dispute.)

Why did the papers treat the fuel protesters so gently? Financially, car advertising is an important source of newspaper income. Ideologically, journalists sensed that readers' sympathies were engaged – until the empty forecourts became a cause of inconvenience. Commercially, publishing is a business and business generally dislikes taxes.

Another much-repeated theory is that, with Labour's big majority in Parliament and a weakened Conservative party, editors felt duty bound to oppose the government. This idea gained currency with a report that Paul Dacre, editor of the *Mail*, had told a senior government official, 'We are going to see you off' – a report that Dacre dismissed as 'twaddle'.[50]

A more precise explanation might be that right-of-centre newspapers seized the opportunity, a year before an expected general election, to issue a warning. Although Tony Blair had promised not to raise income tax, the fuel protests were an opportunity to caution him against raising other 'stealth' taxes to compensate. In particular, they were an opportunity to caution Gordon Brown, his likely successor as leader and prime minister.

In that sense, the fuel protesters were footsoldiers in a bigger tax war between Labour and the right-wing press. Newspapers sympathised with the disorder but they did not manufacture it, nor did they help give it formal political expression.

It is clear that the protesters were incredibly effective and that this is a new political phenomenon.

Chris Gibson-Smith, BP's managing director, 15 Sep 2000

Gay Sex Lessons from the *Daily Record*
Background

When members of the Scottish Parliament started work in 1999, sex was the last thing on their minds. They might have been expecting a debate over tuition fees or land reform. But the issue that ignited was not one which had featured in the Holyrood election campaign or the subsequent coalition talks between Labour and the Liberal Democrats. It was a US-style 'family values' row which scarred the new Executive and soured the early days of devolution.

The key role was played not by the Parliament, but by the press. A coalition between the *Daily Record*, a businessman and the Catholic church turned the repeal of Clause 28 into a clash of values which called into question the nature of the 'new Scotland'.

Clause 28 (or 2A as it was known north of the Border) was a law which specifically forbade the 'promotion' of homosexuality by local authorities. A hangover from the Thatcher era, it was designed to prevent Labour councils spending public money on gay and lesbian groups or teaching aids. Although never tested in court, it was seen as offensive by equality campaigners and Labour was committed to repeal.

While that commitment featured in the 1997 UK manifesto, it was not in the 1999 version produced for the Scottish Parliament elections. It did not appear in the 'Partnership Agreement' hammered out between Labour and the Liberal Democrats, or in the Executive's first legislative programme.

In the furore that followed, campaigners made much of these omissions. They attributed repeal entirely to Wendy Alexander, the cabinet member in charge of local government, who announced her intentions in a speech at Glasgow University, also giving the story to the *Daily Record*. She was criticised for not informing the Parliament first. But MSPs had heard of the plan a month earlier from her junior minister, Jackie Baillie. Repeal would be 'widely welcomed in Scotland', one Labour MSP declared – with what, in retrospect, was more confidence than judgement. Ms Baillie's words were not reported, however – unlike Ms Alexander's.

A number of commentators questioned whether the repeal of Section 28 should be a priority for the new Parliament. The *Daily Mail*, which was producing a Scottish edition in response to devolution, deplored the Executive's move as 'posturing'. Under the headline 'Gay sex lessons for Scots schools', the Labour-supporting *Daily Record* predicted 'an enormous backlash from parents and religious groups'.[51]

But the *Record*, while warning against 'another unnecessary blunder', gave Ms Alexander space to explain why Section 28 'legitimises intolerance and prejudice'. Its editorial column was less hostile than the *Mail*'s, merely observing that the Executive should beware of 'another unnecessary blunder'. The following day it reported: 'Gay gamble pays off: plans get widespread approval.'

In mid-December Tom Brown, an influential commentator with strong Labour links, wrote a strongly worded column in the *Record* – headlined 'Insanity clause perverting the cause of democracy' – warning that children could be exposed to 'corrupting smut' if Section 28 were repealed.[52]

Brian Souter, owner of the bus company Stagecoach, happened to see the column and was appalled by what he read. Souter, a committed evangelical Christian with four children of his own, contacted his PR adviser, Jack Irvine, to discuss mounting a campaign against repeal.

Manufacturing dissent?

Funding presented no problem for Souter, a self-made millionaire. The decision was taken to channel money through the Scottish School

Boards Association. But Irvine, a former editor of the *Scottish Sun*, knew that he needed media support. He rang Martin Clarke, editor of the *Daily Record*, to ask if the paper would back a 'Keep the Clause' campaign. Clarke, while vehemently supportive, wanted to know who was behind the initiative. Scotland being a small place, he quickly hit on Brian Souter's name and put the story on the front page.[53] Thenceforward, as Irvine says, 'a spark was lit and went whoosh'.

The following day, Souter gave an interview to Tom Brown in which he denied being homophobic ('I do not condemn homosexuals, I respect them as individuals and I respect their rights') but argued that politicians, of all parties, were 'out of tune with how ordinary people feel about this'. He even floated the idea of 'a free vote or a referendum' to show the strength of public feeling.[54]

On 18 January Cardinal Thomas Winning, Scotland's most senior Catholic and archbishop of Glasgow, came out in support of Souter, describing homosexuality as 'perverted' and appealing to the 'silent majority' to make their voices heard. This polarised the debate. Gay groups urged a boycott of Souter's buses and of trains run by Virgin, in which he had a stake. Donald Dewar, the First Minister, defended the decision to scrap the clause. A *Record* poll, published on 19 January, showed 66 per cent in favour of keeping it. The launch of the Souter campaign imploded when it emerged that some of the celebrities whose support it claimed, such as the Glasgow chef Nick Nairn and Jim Kerr of Simple Minds, actually favoured repeal.

Irvine and Souter lunched with editors in Glasgow and secured the backing of the *Sun* and the *Daily Mail*, although the *Sunday Mail*, sister paper to the *Record*, was actively hostile. The *Mirror*, which is owned by the same company but has a fraction of the *Record*'s readership – the *Record* was selling around 600,000 copies at the time – backed the Executive, as did the *Scotsman* and the *Herald*.

From then on, the war was fought out in the press. Irvine fed regular stories to friendly papers. Usually he was the 'spokesman' quoted but one or two other names featured regularly, including officers of the Scottish School Boards Association (SSBA) and a member of the Church of Scotland's board of social responsibility –

although both the Kirk and the SSBA were internally split over Section 28. Bashir Mann from the Muslim Council of Great Britain and a spokesman for Cardinal Winning were also quoted. The campaign, according to one journalist who covered the story, 'was a loose collection of people, not a forum that held meetings. We just rang them every day.'[55]

The political parties were pushed into the background. The Scottish Conservatives, who opposed repeal, were upstaged by Souter's initiative and barely figured in the campaign. Labour, the Liberal Democrats and the Scottish Nationalist Party – which had taken money from Souter in the past but now described him as 'a private citizen' – continued to back repeal, with one or two rebels. The cabinet itself was divided, as dissident Labour ministers pressed for a compromise to reassure parents on sex education. But it was the tabloid press which fuelled the fire, framing the issue in terms of protecting children and routinely using the phrase 'gay sex lessons' as a synonym for repeal. 'There wouldn't have been a campaign without the *Record*,' says Irvine.

The *Mail* and the *Record* cooperated closely on the story, with their editors, Martin Clarke and Ramsay Smith, speaking almost every day. Clarke, who lost his job shortly after the Section 28 controversy, later went to work at the *Mail on Sunday*. Smith, after a spell at the *Scotsman*, joined Jack Irvine's PR company.

Both papers, for example, reported a poll showing that rank-and-file trade unionists disagreed with the Scottish TUC, which backed repeal. Both reported a legal opinion, commissioned by the Christian Institute, that parents could challenge sex education lessons under the European Convention on Human Rights – a story picked up by only one other paper in Scotland. Only the *Mail* and the *Record* bothered to record that *War Cry*, the Salvation Army newspaper, had come out against repeal.[56]

Souter's masterstroke, however, was not to co-opt the tabloid press: that had been done before. What made this campaign different, and threatening, was his decision to fund a referendum. Overnight, he was transformed from a rich man crying in the wilderness to a protagonist of DIY democracy. Ministers, already on the defensive, ran the risk of sounding sour as they dismissed what Wendy Alexander called 'a glorified opinion poll'.

Labour had welcomed the idea of a protest referendum when it was used against the Thatcher government. In 1994 the Labour-run Strathclyde regional council organised a poll to test public opinion on the transfer of water services to a quango, securing a 71 per cent turnout and a 97 per cent 'No' vote.

But the Souter referendum was not local but nationwide; not public but private; not municipally led but media-driven. The *Record* was principal publicist as well as chief campaigner. See-sawing between public information ('No matter what your position on this subject, we urge you to vote') and outright partisanship ('Keep voting, they're on the run'), the paper charted day-by-day developments of a running story in which it had a role.[57]

This posed a dilemma for its rivals. The *Mail* stayed in step with the *Record*, maintaining its support for Keep the Clause ('Make sure you use your vote'). The *Sun* was supportive but sparing in its coverage; the *Mirror* was sparing but hostile. The *Sunday Mail*, the *Record*'s sister paper, was consistently critical, finding fault with the way the referendum was run ('Trash poll already a shambles'), and accusing Souter of 'an ever-more-desperate attempt to buy into the laws of this country'.[58]

Like the Belgian press before the White March, the *Record* encouraged turnout by building a sense of confidence and momentum. 'Your votes have flooded in,' it reported. 'Labour head for a hammering in Clause 28 poll'; 'Poll chiefs expect a late rush on Clause 28.'[59]

Despite the use of an old electoral register, which resulted in ballot papers being sent to the dead and younger voters being missed, more than a million people returned their forms, of whom 87 per cent were in favour of keeping Section 28. This was, as experts pointed out, a relatively low turnout – one in three of the voting population – and skewed towards opponents of repeal. But in a country of five million people, it was an impressive result.

By the time of the referendum, however, the focus had shifted from keeping Clause 28 to enshrining marriage in sex education lessons. According to Jack Irvine, Souter realised that ministers would not capitulate on repeal, but might concede safeguards against what he saw as promoting homosexuality in the classroom. This was reflected in a *Record* editorial on 12 May: 'If the government is hell-bent on repealing Clause 28, they must be forced to put something meaningful in its place – a declaration of support for heterosexual marriage as the norm and a clear and enforceable ban on the teaching of homosexuality in schools.'

The result was a classic political fudge, with much to-ing and fro-ing over the legal force of the guidelines that were eventually issued. These specified that children should be encouraged to 'appreciate the value of commitment in relationships and partnerships, including the value placed on marriage by religious groups and others in society'.[60] Cardinal Winning called it 'a victory for common sense'.

Outcomes

The short-term effects were minimal. Parliament repealed Section 2A on 21 June, by 99 votes to 17. Brian Souter, having spent £2 million, went back to his business, which had been suffering and required attention. One of his executive directors was arrested for soliciting a male prostitute in the US.

Despite media speculation, Mr Souter did not set up a 'family values' party to contest the general election; nor did he decide to back 'pro-marriage' candidates from the mainstream parties. No parent has yet brought a legal challenge under the guidelines he fought for.

South of the Border, Section 28 was not repealed until three years later. In this case the resistance came from Parliament, specifically from the Lords, where the charge was led by the Conservative peer Baroness Young. The clause became a touchstone for Tory modernisers when Michael Portillo, unsuccessful candidate for the party leadership in 2001, committed himself to repeal.

For some in Scotland, the Lords rebellions – and the tougher sex education guidelines that were hammered out in consequence – made the case for a revising second chamber north of the Border. It was striking that the Westminster opposition, while strong, was more decorous for being expressed through conventional channels. Perhaps as a result, the press coverage of repeal in England and Wales was not so pugnacious or sustained.

Part of what happened in Scotland may be attributed to personalities. Cardinal Winning took a far more belligerent stand in defence of Section 28 than his English counterparts, Cardinal Hume and later Cardinal Cormac Murphy O'Connor. Wendy Alexander was a passionate and relatively inexperienced politician who believed that repealing Section 28 would be symbolic of the new Scotland. In England and Wales, repeal was handled by David Blunkett, a more cautious figure known for his conservative views on sexual morality. (He later resigned from the cabinet over a relationship with a married woman.)

But there is a sense in which the row over Section 28 may have been a consequence of devolution. Home rule campaigners had assumed that once there was a parliament, the enlightened collectivism of the Scots would shine through. Instead, Scotland, its political culture no longer diluted by being ruled as part of the UK, came up short against its own fears and prejudice.

The fact that the new parliament lacked control over tax, immigration, defence and welfare may be another reason why a moral issue took on such importance. With the big questions of security and redistribution out of range, the politics of behaviour offered a new dividing line.

At the same time, the newspaper market north of the Border had become highly competitive, with London-based papers like the *Daily Mail* investing in Scottish editions with their own staff and news agendas. The parliament had proved disappointing as a source of news, leaving political correspondents starving for a story. While the *Record*'s desire to maintain its market position might help explain why it turned so savagely on Labour, the campaign did not raise its sales.

But was the story whipped up by journalists? Masterminded by Souter and Irvine? Or precipitated by the Executive? One school of thought, embracing politicians of all parties, blamed ministers for awaking passions that would otherwise have slept. 'I have to ask myself why the matter was raised at all,' remarked Annabel Goldie, deputy Scottish Conservative leader, in a parliamentary debate. 'There was certainly no public appetite in Scotland for raising it.'[61] The Executive was burned by the reaction. In vain did ministers point out that they had conducted a consultation process which found 75 per cent of respondents in favour of repeal: opponents argued it had been 'hi-jacked' by the gay lobby.

One long-term effect was to make Scottish politicians nervous of anything involving morality or family values. The Civil Partnerships Bill, which would have allowed same-sex couples to register their relationship, was sent down to Westminster even though the Scottish Parliament had the legislative power to handle it. The Executive also showed caution over gay adoption and sex education in schools, issues on which the Catholic church remained vigilant long after press interest had waned.

But the real significance of the campaign was to threaten representative democracy head-on. The press not only championed public opinion: it had intervened directly in politics to set the terms of debate.

A campaign without precedent in British public life.

Wendy Alexander on Keep the Clause, 21 Jun 2000

4. The new opposition?

For Robert Putnam, communitarian guru, they are 'media events'. The sociologist Zymunt Bauman writes of 'spectacular one-off explosions'. Sidney Tarrow, an expert on protest movements, refers to 'brief and exhilarating performances'.

Instant protest is evanescent. Like a passing storm, it comes out of the blue and vanishes into the air. Climactic conditions must be right or, as the fuel protesters and the White Marchers found with their failed attempts, it will dissipate in drizzle. Once the immediate crisis is past, politicians breathe a sigh of relief and get on with business as usual.

They take their cue from the media, which contributes to the sense of overnight irrelevance. One day every paper had the fuel protests on the front page; the next, they had vanished. Jobs change often in journalism: attention spans and memories are short. Editors and news editors decide – often arbitrarily – that they have 'had enough' of an issue.

Politicians also feel free to dismiss protest because it usually comes from the other side – the anti-war demonstrations being an interesting exception. Academics have shown what common sense suggests, that left-wing protest increases under right-wing governments and vice versa.[62] In Tony Blair's first term, with a big Labour majority and a weak opposition, the incentive for extra-parliamentary protest was high. But ministers, secure in their electoral mandate, were sufficiently confident to face it down. 'We cannot and we will not alter government policy on petrol through blockades and pickets,' the Prime Minister told the fuel protesters. 'That's not the way to make policy in Britain, and as far as I'm concerned it never will be.'[63]

If politicians have the backing of the ballot box, surely manufactured dissent can safely be dismissed? None of the recent campaigns achieved their ostensible goals. Parents do not have access to the register of paedophiles. Section 28 was repealed. A ban on foxhunting was finally passed in November 2004, despite repeated opposition from the Lords.

But the press-protest axis achieves long-term results by framing the political agenda. The repeal of Section 28, which Scottish ministers saw a civil rights issue, became a debate about the protection of children and the social standing of marriage. The banning of hunting, which Labour MPs saw in terms of animal welfare, was re-cast as a struggle between town and country, statists and libertarians.

The *News of the World*'s campaign against paedophiles highlighted the intensity of public opinion and created a more punitive climate. The alliance between fuel protesters, the *Sun* and the *Mail* made petrol tax rises politically impossible by promoting the image of motorists as a martyred class. The double-act of Keep the Clause and the *Daily Record* helped stall repeal of Section 28 south of the Border and deterred Scottish ministers from further reforms relating to sexual morality or family values. The Countryside Alliance, backed by the *Daily Telegraph* and the *Mail*, not only delayed a foxhunting ban – assisted by the Lords – but forced an urban-minded Labour government to pay attention to rural issues.

What should worry the mainstream parties is that they were not at the eye of the storm. While many pro-hunting and fuel protesters were natural Tory voters, these were not issues that William Hague, then party leader, had targeted. A few front-bench Tories were calling for lower fuel duty in the summer of 2000, but the top team was preoccupied with Europe, asylum and crime. Hague and his lieutenants fought shy of the 'Sarah's Law' campaign, and their colleagues in Scotland were slow to appreciate the force of Keep the Clause. Theirs was an insignificant role compared with that of the *Mail*, the *News of the World* and the *Record*.

Why press activism?

What do newspapers gain by opting to join protest movements, rather than merely reporting them? And what are the implications of today's dash to the virtual picket line?

In a competitive market where sales are declining, newspapers cast about for causes with which their readers can engage and identify. It is no coincidence that Rebekah Wade was a new editor with a mission to drive circulation up at the time of the *News of the World*'s 'For Sarah' campaign. The *Daily Mail* increased sales with its 2003 ballot for a referendum on the proposed EU constitution. But dissent cannot be relied on to add sales, as the *Record* found with Section 28. Circulation is far more likely to be affected by price cuts and special offers, by sport, or by big events like Diana's death and the Asian tsunami disaster.

The aggressive press activism of recent years may owe something to the challenge of the internet, a medium uniquely suited to mobilisation. Protesters themselves – from anti-globalisers to militant Christians – use the Web to organise. But a newspaper, if it shouts loud enough, is a powerful ally.

This is a rare example where, in Britain at least, the press has an advantage over television. While the camera is the natural medium through which to evoke sympathy for divorced fathers or snuffling foxhounds, broadcasting rules prescribe that the screen reporter cannot take sides like his print counterpart. Newspapers, unconstrained apart from the laws of libel and contempt, can denigrate or champion as they please.

At the same time as being more activist, the press is more ideologically footloose. Since Richard Desmond bought the *Daily Express* in 2000, it has swung from Labour to Tory, from pro- to anti-EU, from famine relief for Africa to Aids tests for immigrants.

The *Daily Record* was a rock-solid Labour-supporting paper before

Section 28. Yet commercial pressures and the search for a unique selling point were enough to make it turn against Labour on this issue. In the same way, the *Daily Mail*'s campaign against genetically modified food has put the paper in sympathy with all manner of unlikely red and green activists.

If newspapers are keeping odd company, it is in the interests of opposing the government. Labour's majority and the Tories' weakness has caused frustration even to left-of-centre papers like the *Guardian* and the *Daily Mirror*, let alone their dominant right-of-centre counterparts.

To whom should an irate editor give his backing? The *Daily Mail*'s Paul Dacre has described the Blair government as 'manipulative, dictatorial and slightly corrupt'. Yet his chairman, Viscount Rothermere, calls the Blairs 'remarkable people' and says the Tories should not count on the *Mail*'s endorsement.[64]

Rupert Murdoch's papers, which came out for Blair in 2001, backed the Prime Minister on Iraq but vehemently oppose him on tax and Europe. Irwin Stelzer, a consultant and columnist for News International, recently accused Gordon Brown of 'laying such a heavy tax burden on Britain that he is dooming it to third-class status', which makes ideological sense of the *Sun*'s sympathy for the fuel protesters.

Stelzer also predicted that if Mr Blair signed the new European constitution, his successor would have no more power than a local councillor.[65] In the forthcoming referendum campaign, the News International stable will be campaigning for a 'No' vote alongside UKIP and Robert Kilroy-Silk's new party, Veritas.

With the Tories weak and divided, it is natural that right-wing newspapers should look for new protagonists to aid and support. Protesters have become accessories in an issue-by-issue struggle between a left-of-centre government and a right-of-centre press.

This was not the case under the Conservatives, when protesters' goals were less likely to coincide with editorial policies. No newspaper endorsed the poll tax resisters, for example. The poll tax was scrapped not because of the non-payment campaign and the riots in Trafalgar

Square, but because of splits inside the Conservative Party.

Even under Labour, there are unspoken ideological limits to what the press will support, especially if there is any taint of violence or threat to free speech. The anti-globalisation and animal rights movements are important to many younger voters yet command scant sympathy from newspapers. When Christian groups demanded that the BBC cancel its showing of *Jerry Springer – the opera*, the *Mail* at first backed them – only to change gear sharply when BBC executives started receiving threats.[66]

Where British newspapers are most comfortable is in resisting attempts by government to change the status quo, be it through banning hunting, repealing Section 28 or trying to raise taxes. On issues like these, the press has joined the picket line as parties limp to catch up. Strains in the system – the slow response times of conventional politics and the lack of a strong opposition – have created a vacuum where the media can champion short-term and often highly sectional interests.

'What's wrong with that?' a robust editor will ask. The fourth estate has always acted as a gauge of public opinion, and it is not newspapers' fault if the headline-writers make a better job of it than MPs. What is new is the conjunction of interests, and the way newspapers are using protest movements as a battering ram against elected politicians.

5. Referendum-itis

In a democracy, one of the irreducible functions of the state is to conduct elections. The trend towards press plebiscites poses a dual challenge: to the government as arbiter of public choices, and to politicians as representatives of public opinion.

During the run-up to the privately funded Section 28 referendum in May 2000, ministers took care to re-affirm their own legitimacy. 'I have absolutely no intention of abdicating responsibility to any opinion poll,' declared Donald Dewar, the First Minister, as Wendy Alexander attacked Brian Souter's 'cheque-book democracy'. But the *Record* was able to claim that the Souter referendum was being held only because the proper authorities would not oblige. An ICM poll[67] found that 74 per cent believed the Scottish Parliament should hold a referendum on the repeal of Section 28.

Referendums were still considered a foreign import when Harold Wilson renegotiated Britain's membership of the European Economic Community in 1975. Roy Jenkins was among those who objected to 'the importation of the then novel device . . . into our constitutional arrangements'.[68]

By the end of the century, however, the idea had taken root. Under Tony Blair, Labour had held referendums on whether there should be a Scottish parliament, a Welsh assembly, and a London mayor. It was committed to a referendum on the European single currency, and dumped a manifesto pledge for another on voting reform. Councils were encouraged to hold referendums on council tax levels and on directly elected mayors.

Thus the plebiscite habit, always a convenient media device, became a familiar part of political life. The distinction between direct and representative democracy was beginning to break down, and the press took advantage of that.

The *Mail*, the *Sun* and the European constitution

Nowhere was this more clearly illustrated than in the *Daily Mail*'s campaign for a referendum on the European constitution drawn up under the auspices of Valery Giscard d'Estaing. Eurosceptics warmed to the idea of a referendum after the Danes rejected the euro in 2000 and the Irish knocked back the Nice Treaty in 2001. It came to be seen as a way of combating out-of-touch Euro-elites with federalist ambitions.

The *Mail* launched its campaign in May 2003 with the front-page headline 'There must be a referendum'. In an editorial headed 'Blueprint for tyranny'[69] it forecast an end to British identity and national sovereignty if the constitution came into force. Ministers were at first unbending, insisting that MPs should be the ones to scrutinise and ratify the treaty. Peter Hain, Britain's negotiator at the convention, dismissed the constitution as a 'tidying up exercise' and said that if people didn't like it they could vote against it in the 2004 European elections. Tony Blair maintained that he saw 'no case' for a referendum.[70]

Calling this 'The Great Betrayal', the *Mail* arranged its own referendum instead. This was portrayed as a rescue mission ('*Mail* gives everyone a voice in Europe') and 'an exercise unprecedented in newspaper history'. The referendum was held on a Thursday, 'because that is the traditional day that polling takes place in this country'.[71] Readers were invited to vote by post, text message, or at ballot boxes placed in newsagents, petrol garages and other retailers like the pub chain Wetherspoons. Celebrity endorsements from Carol Vorderman and Jilly Cooper added a touch of glamour.

At the same time, the *Sun* was running a campaign of its own ('Give us a euro-vote if you dare, Mr Blair'), including a telephone poll that showed 159,000 voters – 92 per cent of the total – in favour of a referendum.

Mr Blair, while not changing position, began to defend the constitution. He framed the dispute more starkly as a question of whether Britain should stay in the EU – 'an argument precipitated by you guys and your campaign', he told the *Mail*.[72] With the *Sun* in hot pursuit, the *Mail* used now-familiar tactics to build up a sense of momentum. On 5 June it reported a 'fantastic start' as 'Thousands in a rush to join our referendum'. On 6 June: 'Votes pour in'. On 11 June, the day before the referendum: 'Excitement is building across Britain on the eve of the *Daily Mail*'s unique referendum day'.

Of the 1.7 million people who voted, 89 per cent were in favour of a referendum. (This was, as the *Mail* was quick to point out, the same number as voted in the referendum on the London mayor, and half a million more than in the referendum on the Welsh Assembly.) An ICM poll, prudently commissioned by the *Mail* in case its voters were dismissed as a self-selecting sample, came out with an 88 per cent 'yes'. The results were published on the same day that the government announced it would hold referendums on English regional government.[73] 'Even at its arrogant worst, New Labour cannot ignore this poll,' the *Mail* declared. Ten months later, Tony Blair announced that that a referendum would be held on the constitution after all, prompting the *Sun* to tell its readers 'EU did it!'[74]

Would the Labour leader have decided to go for a referendum anyway? Press reports suggested that Jack Straw, the Foreign Secretary, played an influential role in changing the Prime Minister's mind. Practical politics intervened when the Tories and the Liberal Democrats agreed to unite in amending the treaty legislation to insist on a referendum. This may have prompted Blair to take the initiative rather than be seen to bow under pressure.

Others identified the influence of Rupert Murdoch, whose aide-de-camp, Irwin Stelzer, had visited the Prime Minister in March. He is supposed to have warned Blair that Murdoch's papers would not support him in the general election – as they had in 2001 – without a commitment to a referendum. Stelzer himself dismissed this as 'implausible'.[75] Jack Straw, the Foreign Secretary, also denied it, saying his views were formed by talking to his constituents. 'It was not The Sun "wot did it", it was the people in Blackburn.'[76]

People in Blackburn, however, may well have been influenced by papers like the *Sun* and the *Mail*. Tony Blair certainly thought so, referring in his Commons statement to 'myths . . . political and media'.[77] Examples he cited were that Brussels would set tax rates and take control of North Sea oil, stories which both papers had featured. Peter Hain, then Leader of the Commons, put the point more forcefully: 'You've got Eurosceptic papers that are just peddling lies the whole time, of course people are going to want a referendum.'[78]

Press-protest and direct democracy

There are two obvious objections to press plebiscites such as those organised by Keep the Clause and the *Mail*. One is that they arrogate to private individuals or corporations a function that should be reserved for the state. Press publishers are selling products and have interests of their own that could skew the way they approach a ballot. The other is that a press plebiscite confuses roles which ought to be separate. The newspaper is not just holding the election but campaigning for one side.

In the world of politics, great efforts are normally made to build Chinese walls between the government that is holding the referendum and the cause it is supporting. In the case of a referendum on the single currency or the European Constitution, the independent Election Commission would look at how the question was worded and nominate a 'yes' and a 'no' campaign to receive state funding.

The *Guardian* sent a team of 'election observers' to monitor the *Mail*'s referendum. Pronouncing it 'totally flawed' – they found individuals stuffing boxes with as many as 30 ballot papers – the team asked the executive editor what efforts had been made to present both sides of the argument. 'None whatsoever,' was the reply.[79]

Both the *Record* and the *Mail* were careful to argue that an official referendum would be preferable. 'We had to arrange the referendum because the PM is refusing to hold one,' explained a Mail editorial.[80]

The assumption is that protest is acceptable if the government is 'not listening'.

The public is inclined to agree, according to polls carried out by ICM in 2000; 81 per cent felt that 'if governments don't listen, peaceful protests and demonstrations are a legitimate way of expressing people's concern'. Asked about specific protests, 65 per cent thought that pro-hunting demonstrations were 'definitely' or 'perhaps' justified, a figure that rose to 74 per cent for the fuel protests.[81]

The phrase 'not listening' is cited repeatedly as a justification for press intervention in politics. But it obscures the question: does listening to people mean acceding to their demands? ICM found poll respondents confused on this point: 35 per cent strongly agreed or tended to agree with the statement, 'In a parliamentary democracy, governments should not change policies in response to protests, blockades or demonstrations'; 39 per cent strongly disagreed or tended to disagree, and the remainder – just over a quarter – did not know.

The run-up to the Iraq war also saw the government accused of 'not listening' ('Mr Blair, are you listening?'; 'Tony Blair and Jack Straw must listen'; 'Labour does not listen'). In a variant on the theme, it was accused of listening to the wrong people. 'Unrepresentative voices from Westminster and from out-of-touch parts of the media have dominated this debate,' editorialised the *Independent*.[82]

Although most British newspapers backed the war, the *Mirror*, the *Guardian* and the *Independent* supported the protesters, while the *Mail*, perhaps mindful of its high female readership – women were more likely to oppose the war – was doubtful. None organised a ballot, but the question of a referendum did arise, both before and after the Iraq vote in the House of Commons on 18 March. An ICM poll commissioned by the *Mirror* and GMTV found that 62 per cent wanted a referendum on the war.[83] Ten thousand people in Liverpool asked for one in a petition conveyed to Downing Street by the Labour MP Bob Wareing.[84]

The California syndrome

In the case of Iraq, the Prime Minister felt strong enough to resist public opinion. In the case of the European constitution, he did not. The cases differ in that one involved real people on the streets of Britain, while the other was a press campaign that articulated – and, arguably, helped shape – public opinion in a virtual forum.

But what if circumstances had been different? Supposing Rupert Murdoch's newspapers had opposed the war, and Tony Blair's Commons majority had been smaller? Would the combined effect of the street protests and the press campaign have been enough to change the Prime Minister's mind?

Another scenario, easier to imagine. After a violent terrorist attack, or a particularly nasty murder, the *Sun* decides to hold a referendum on the reintroduction of hanging. Its campaign is backed up by the *Mail*, albeit in loftier tones. An overwhelming 'yes' vote leaves MPs in the uncomfortable position of being cast as elitist appeasers.

These are prospects that elected politicians need to consider. Conventional electoral systems may not suit a future in which sovereignty is pooled, voters are impatient, and technology allows swift expressions of opinion. The growing use of plebiscites on television shows like *Big Brother* and *Pop Idol* is acclimatising a whole generation to the idea of simple choices, snap decisions and quick results.

The US is often invoked in discussions of direct democracy – 24 states allow for citizen initiatives but California is the best known, both for the number and the intensity with which they are fought. They have included Proposition 13, which limited property taxes, and Proposition 187, which outlawed the provision of health and education services to illegal immigrants.

Peter Schrag, who writes on direct democracy in California, calls his state 'an urgent cautionary tale'.[85] He describes the way in which corporate interests such as the insurance industry effectively buy their way onto the ballot by hiring professionals to collect the number of signatures needed to get their question included.

Schrag also identifies a vicious circle whereby voters, mistrusting politicians, seek to tie their hands through ballot measures – limiting the legislature's ability to tax and spend, for example, or restricting the length of time that members can serve. The result is that elected representatives have little room for manoeuvre in tackling state problems, further aggravating public frustration. Yet Californians appear to like their perverse system, the most frequent complaint being that the laws they vote for are not properly enforced; 44 per cent volunteer that referendums 'give people a voice'.[86]

That is exactly what UK newspapers say they are trying to do in the face of government obduracy. As turnout falls and mistrust of politicians grows, pressure for greater use of referendums is likely to increase. Research shows that people are more likely to support the idea of direct democracy if they are dissatisfied with political parties or the way democracy is working.[87]

Even the framers of the proposed European constitution have turned to direct democracy as a way of bridging the EU's 'democratic deficit', with a clause requiring the commission to back a law if a million citizens petition for it. Yet suspicion of direct democracy is widespread in British political life. 'I hate referendums,' observed Chris Patten, former Conservative cabinet minister and European commissioner, just after Tony Blair agreed to hold one on the EU constitution. 'They are deeply illiberal. They undermine parliamentary democracy.'[88]

The animating fear is more than a legitimate concern that private money and special interests could influence a vote. It is a fear of what people actually want, or could be made to want. A referendum on Section 28 would probably have meant the law staying on the statute book. The shadow of capital punishment clouds attitudes to direct democracy among the liberal elite in Britain.

Schrag describes California as being in 'a condition of permanent neo-populism'. Yet ballot initiatives do not necessarily yield 'illiberal' results. Oregon rejected one initiative restricting gay rights and passed another allowing 'assisted suicide', or euthanasia. California's Mendocino County recently voted to ban GM crops. They may, however, yield ill-considered results which assert the majority over the minority, the short over the long term, the lay person's gut reaction over the expert opinion. A referendum on 'Sarah's Law' might have resulted in a 'yes' vote, creating conditions in which paedophiles went underground. A referendum on hospital closures would probably yield a 'no', yet experts maintain that big specialist centres are preferable to small local hospitals.

There is no inherent reason why direct democracy should elicit ill-considered or ignorant reactions. Experiments such as citizens' juries, or the 'deliberation day' proposed by the American political theorist James Fishkin, seek to ensure that a referendum would be more than just a cross on a ballot paper. But the media, by encouraging knee-jerk reactions and snap judgements, fulfils the worst expectations of those who mistrust direct democracy. As the French sociologist Pierre Bourdieu puts it, 'A perverse form of direct democracy can come into play when the media act in a way that is calculated to mobilise the public.' When journalists articulate unreflective and emotional demands, he argues, they reinforce the tendency of politicians to give in to the majority. By strengthening the hand of demagogues, the press undermines politicians' authority 'as guardians of collective values'.[89]

So there are two possible views of press-protest: as a way of short-circuiting direct democracy, or a way of articulating opinions ignored by political elites. A referendum on fuel prices could have forced Gordon Brown to cut excise duty, skewing decisions about taxation. On the other hand, a referendum on the European constitution will give the public a chance to vote on far-reaching changes which would otherwise be signed off in their name.

The problem with condemning the press is that they are going with the flow of what people seem to want. Californians aren't the only ones in favour of referendums. In the UK, 77 per cent agree that certain issues should be put to the popular vote. The same proportion back a system that could force the government to hold a referendum with a petition of, say, a million signatures.[90]

Direct democracy is a product for which there is demand. Newspapers are selling it.

6. Giving voice, shrinking space

The thwarting of public opinion

In April 2002, police were called to a farm in the Scottish Highlands where a field of genetically modified oilseed rape had been vandalised. It was the latest episode in a saga of local and national resistance to GM crop trials which inspired a plot line in *The Archers* and saw an organic farmer put in jail.

At every stage and every level, public opinion was thwarted. Tony Blair commissioned a nationwide consultation, *GM Nation*, which reported in September 2003 that 'the mood ranged from caution and doubt, through suspicion and scepticism, to hostility and rejection'. He ignored it, giving the go-ahead to commercial growing of genetically modified maize.

In the Highlands, local campaigners drew up petitions for an end to the trials and sent them to the Scottish Parliament. The transport and environment committee backed the petitioners. But the rural affairs minister, Ross Finnie, insisted that his hands were tied by a European Union directive. Finnie was a Liberal Democrat minister in a coalition government. His party supported a moratorium on GM crop trials, a policy reaffirmed by the Scottish Liberal Democrats shortly after the farm was vandalised. Yet still it appeared there was nothing he could do.

The story goes some way to explain why single-issue protest movements are on the rise. For what should the concerned citizen have done? The parliamentary route was fruitless; the party route was blocked. Scotland's new devolved parliament, set up to bring decision-making closer to home, was powerless to change the fate of a field a few hundred miles away. No wonder people feel thwarted and impatient for results.

Now imagine if there had been a newspaper backing the protesters. In fact there was, but it was not aligned in time or place with what was happening in the Highlands. The *Daily Mail*, with its unerring feel for the pulse of Middle England, chose to campaign against GM under the label 'Frankenstein foods'. Headlines like 'Is GM the new thalidomide?' and 'No crops safe if GM goes ahead' left the paper's position in no doubt, although it showed more interest in the Home Counties' activism of Jude Law and Camilla Parker Bowles's son Tom than in vigils farther north.[91]

The *Mail* only started campaigning in earnest after the row in the Highlands had subsided, so in this case the press-protest symbiosis did not occur. But it is worth speculating what would have happened had the paper held a ballot on GM crops – and whether the Prime Minister would have taken more notice of that than of the government's own consultation.

The prospect of commercially grown GM crops receded in the spring of 2004 – not because ministers responded to public opinion, but because the biotech companies did. BayerCropScience, the firm responsible for making the first approved variety of maize, withdrew the seed from the market shortly after the government gave approval for it to be grown in Britain.

Identity politics and the party system

The resistance to GM crops is a good example of what ignites contemporary protest. It combines fear of the unknown, mistrust of new technology, a desire to protect 'nature' and a reluctance to take politicians' assurances on trust. But – apart from organic farmers who stand to lose from possible contamination – it is not about economic self-interest. Most of the protests examined here could be classed as 'post-materialist' or 'identity politics', in the sense that they focus on cultural values rather than material conditions. The exception might be the fuel blockades, which looked like a tax revolt but carried connotations of the 'freedom to drive'.

The pro-hunting movement is essentially about defending a pastime, a way of life. Vigilantism against paedophiles and Keep the Clause campaign are 'moral panics', in which an event (like Sarah Payne's death) or a perceived risk (such as children being indoctrinated with pro-gay teaching) activates a whole set of anxieties.

Some sociologists diagnose these cultural protests as resistance movements against an invasive state, the product of insecurity in a fast-changing world. Others, more optimistic, see them as new forms of self-expression by assertive citizens who can afford to worry about more than where their next meal is coming from.[92] Either way, the main parties are ill-placed to respond. Based around broad coalitions of shared economic or class interests, they are not geared to fighting on single-issue platforms or, despite their spin-doctors' efforts, keeping pace with the drama of media and activist campaigning.

Insofar as hunting is a party issue, it is a Conservative issue. Indeed, the majority of Countryside Alliance marchers – 82 per cent, according to a poll taken on the 2002 London march – are Tory voters.[93] William Hague and Iain Duncan Smith turned up to demonstrate. But it was never their show, to the point where the *Sun* demanded 'Where are the Tories when we need them?'[94]

Resistance to genetically modified foods would belong naturally to the Liberal Democrats, yet they never took ownership of the issue. In Scotland, they were constrained by their position in coalition with Labour; nationally, Charles Kennedy has focused on Iraq and public services. The Greens were better placed, but had only one MSP at the height of the row, and no MPs at Westminster.

Parties have not yet found their way in the landscape being churned up by the new media-protest axis. It is demoralising for them to be upstaged by ad hoc networks of activists and noisy newspapers. Policy forums may toil for months on consultation documents, but it only takes a handful of campaigners and a newspaper to stop a hospital being closed or prompt a crackdown on asylum-seekers whose claims have been rejected. Parties come under pressure to adopt simple, issue-based positions – cut petrol prices, no GM crops – but must then grapple with complex policy details and trade-offs, which makes them look flat-footed and resistant. The effect is to weaken their standing and discourage citizens from seeing them as a way of getting their voices heard.

Who rules? Symbiosis and the misattribution of power

I have tried to show that the relationship between protest and the media is symbiotic. Campaigners need coverage to publicise their grievance – and increase the chance of a quick response. Newspapers are in search both of stories to cover and entry-points into political debate.

Taken separately, these goals are wholly legitimate. Taken together, the compound effect may be to distort, undermine or paralyse our political culture. Protesters want instant attention from government; newspapers want to increase circulation and advance the interests of their editors or owners. The resulting combination takes on a life of its own, forcing politicians to react, and shaping policy choices. Nobody owns this effect; it emerges from the public mixing of volatile ingredients.

The *Sun* and the *Mail* did not create anger over petrol prices, but they campaigned for months to rouse indignation and direct it at the government rather than the oil companies or OPEC. Though they could not manufacture a protest (witness the failure of the 'Dump the Pump' boycott), these papers lent legitimacy to the blockades when they happened, ignoring environmental arguments about pollution and global warming. The *Telegraph* and the *Mail* did not manufacture indignation over foxhunting, but they helped the Countryside Alliance evoke a gulf between rural and urban life when the countryside's most acute problems, such as lack of affordable housing, apply equally to cities.

The Section 28 affair showed that a protest movement does not require thousands of people on the streets: it can be reduced to an astute PR man and a friendly newspaper. Moreover, as the *Record* established and the *Mail* confirmed, it can be crystallised in a referendum campaign that mimics the formal process of democracy. There will come a day when electoral turnout will be juxtaposed uncomfortably with a newspaper campaign – in the way that the *Mail* compared its 1.7 million voters with the numbers voting in the referendums on the Welsh assembly and the London mayor – and suffer from the comparison.

There is nothing intrinsically wrong with democratic debate migrating from political institutions to the media. If it re-animates interest and engages people, especially the young, so much the better. A weblog may be more attractive than a public meeting, a witty headline more enticing than a pompous parliamentary exchange.

The problem is that the media set the terms. Newspapers create an alternative political ecology, a one-party state in which they set the question and campaign on one side only. That might matter less in an industry with more diversity of ownership, but when four groups control 80 per cent of national newspaper circulation in the UK, it makes politics as much a monopoly business as the press.

Manufactured dissent inhabits a domain of simple questions and yes–no answers, where the majority wins and the losers are, *Big Brother*-style, evicted. It is a faster and more responsive system, without room for nuance. It can accommodate the rise and fall of instant parties, like Forza Italia and Pim Fortuyn's List. It allows celebrities to move easily between showbiz and politics, attaching themselves to a cause or to a party, as Robert Kilroy-Silk did with UKIP. It is unabashed by corporate influence, whether exerted by a bus tycoon like Brian Souter or a vertically integrated giant like News International.

What could be lost? The mediating function of politicians, their role as honest brokers. It was the local MP in Portsmouth, Syd Rapson, who helped get a dialogue going between Paulsgrove residents, housing officers and social services. Someone has to perform the thankless task of persuading groups with different interests to talk and compromise – a task that newspapers have no appetite for. Someone has to weigh the price of petrol against the general tax take and the need to cut carbon dioxide emissions.

In diplomacy, the role of intermediaries is valued and admired. Not in domestic politics. All the emphasis is placed on executive action, so that press and public come to demand near-supernatural efficacy. Politicians respond with unrealistic predictions of what they can achieve, creating a closed circuit of frustration and blame. Newspapers paint a misleading picture of where power lies, neglecting to acknowledge what Zygmunt Bauman calls 'the ongoing separation of power from politics'.[95]

Tony Blair did not kill off the cod in the North Sea. Yet when the European Commission tried to conserve the remaining stocks, he was held responsible for a policy which forced fishermen to tie up their boats. Scottish ministers did not scare off American visitors in the lean year of 2001 – terrorism and foot-and-mouth took care of that – yet the press held them responsible for the plight of the tourist industry.

Press-protest attributes Olympian powers to politicians, yet the dominant message is anti-politics. Coverage of Section 28 and the fuel blockades was peppered with references to Labour 'lies', an 'arrogant' government, the 'greed' of the Chancellor. The tone is nihilistic and angry.

Matthew Taylor, an adviser to Tony Blair and former director of the think tank IPPR, argues that newspapers exacerbate a culture of 'infantile rage' which avoids examining contradictory impulses, such as the dislike of pollution and the desire to own a car. The media, he concludes, makes it harder to promote understanding and reconcile different interests in the public sphere.[96]

Media democracy?

Some take the argument to its logical conclusion and contend that politics has been colonised by the press. Thomas Meyer, a German political scientist, has attempted to pin down the phenomenon but the notion is not confined to academia. The Culture Secretary, Tessa Jowell, fears that a 'pressocracy' could fill the vacuum of voter disengagement, while the journalist John Lloyd believes that the media seeks to destroy the credibility and authority of elected politicians.[97]

As we have seen, however, there is a limit to what press-protest can achieve in the face of a determined government with a parliamentary majority. The mass-circulation German newspaper *Bild Zeitung* backed street demonstrations against Chancellor Schroeder's welfare reforms in the autumn of 2004, yet the reforms went through. The test case in Britain could prove to be the referendum on the EU constitution – likely to be a classic instance of manufactured dissent, albeit one that culminates in a state-sponsored referendum rather than a press-sponsored one.

Newspapers are themselves not trusted, so have scant claim to superiority as representatives of public opinion. Surveys by MORI consistently find that whereas 90 per cent of respondents trust doctors to tell the truth, only 20 per cent say the same of journalists – comparable to the 22 per cent who have faith in politicians. A YouGov poll established that people were more likely to trust television journalists or broadsheet newspapers than mid-market or 'red-top' tabloids.[98] In the absence of trust, editors claim market endorsement instead. The *Daily Mail*'s Paul Dacre says he has to face a daily 'general election' in persuading people to buy a copy of his paper.

The difference is that newspapers are transitory and the decision to buy inconsequential. Walter Lippmann compared the press to a searchlight moving restlessly about, 'bringing one episode and then another out of darkness into vision'. It could never, he argued, be a substitute for institutions. 'Men cannot do the work of the world by this light alone. They cannot govern society by episodes, incidents, and eruptions.'[99]

While politicians might envy the spontaneity and directness of manufactured dissent, society needs politics to be slower-burn and longer-term. Manufactured dissent, even as it amplifies demands for action, restricts the scope for dialogue, complexity and compromise.

7. Manufacturing dissent: press and parties in transition

Manufactured dissent is part of politics today, and should be recognised rather than dismissed. It highlights strains in the system, exposing the impotence of parties and the panic of the press in the face of their mutual decline. But it also suggests that democracy is not exhausted. Out there in 'civil society' is an abundance of energy and passion, sometimes destructively expressed, which newspapers magnify and amplify. People may not be interested in voting yet feel strongly – if intermittently – about windfarms, immigration or animal rights.

The American sociologist Albert Hirschman laid out three types of consumer response to institutions: exit, voice and loyalty. Choosing not to vote is a form of exit. Newspapers give voice, by expressing currents of public opinion that the party system can't or won't accommodate. But they do so in an idiom that seems calculated to turn people against politics, reinforcing the inclination to exit.

The ideal would be to give voice, pre-empt exit and trigger loyalty, so that citizens stay inside the civic circle. The verve and indignation that goes into manufacturing dissent has the potential to re-animate and transform politics, aligning it more closely with the issues people care about and channelling infantile rage into grown-up engagement.

Simple policy prescriptions won't work. Just as manufactured dissent is the product of uncoordinated action by different players, constructive responses could come from different places.

Post-modern parties

If parties were doing their job, voters would not feel the need to take to the streets and newspapers would be less inclined to pose as their champions. Not only has Labour been unresponsive in the examples described here: other parties have been slow to spot issues that agitate people, from petrol prices to GM crops, from fair trade to foxhunting.

This is not just a characteristic of Tony Blair's government. A study of the ill-fated community charge, introduced by Margaret Thatcher in her third term, concludes that 'in a perfect world, where parties reflected public opinion faithfully, there would have been no poll tax'. The Tories would never have committed themselves to the poll tax and the opposition would have united against it.[100]

The familiar next step is to argue, as many do, that a truly responsive political system requires electoral reform. Scotland and Wales, with their more proportional systems, have already more single-issue candidates. Dr Jean Turner became an MSP in 2003 after campaigning against hospital closures, channelling a current of opinion that forced a Scotland-wide moratorium and cost the health minister his job. The following year, 12 members of UKIP were elected to the European Parliament on a platform of EU withdrawal, a position unrepresented in mainstream British politics.

Voting reform would offer more choice, but could also exacerbate the trend towards volatile populism evident in other parts of Europe. A greater choice of parties doesn't overcome the problem of demand for an instant response or a sudden backlash against a particular policy. We would have to accept the possibility of a charismatic figure creating a party from a surge of discontent, as Pim Fortuyn co-opted dislike of Muslims and asylum-seekers in the name of Dutch liberal values. The fortunes of Robert Kilroy-Silk could be very different under a proportional system.

But a greater choice of parties doesn't get over the problem of demand for an instant response or a sudden backlash against a particular policy. There is a mismatch between conventional politics, which works on a slow timescale, and press-protest, which is the equivalent of the fast food industry. Nor would voting reform eliminate the axis between protest and the press. Silvio Berlusconi took advantage of the new PR system in Italy – but fashioned his new party, Forza Italia, using his football and media empire.

Parties are struggling to adapt to an era in which people prefer causes to manifestos and networks to clubs. Politicians ponder the attractions of the Royal Society for the Protection of Birds or single-issue coalitions like the debt-relief campaign Jubilee 2000. Some are also trying to improve grassroots dialogue, with varying degrees of success. Labour's pre-2005 election 'Big Conversation', while much derided, sent ministers round the country to take questions at public meetings. In Greece, the opposition party Pasok invited non-members to vote in a primary-style election for its leader, George Papandreou, who is experimenting with a more participatory approach.

The internet, which has scarcely infiltrated formal politics, has the potential to transform this as so many other kinds of social life. Joe Trippi, who managed Howard Dean's campaign for the Democratic presidential nomination, is messianic about the 'grassroots internet insurgency' that activated a nationwide network of supporters – many of them young – and raised unprecedented sums in small donations. Iain Duncan-Smith, the former Tory leader, believes bloggers could help revive the right.[101]

New technology will also make it easier for determined campaigners to penetrate the institutional undergrowth. One website, TheyWorkForYou.com, has a search feature to track everything that has been said in the Commons since 2001 on a particular subject, for example GM crops or *Jerry Springer – the opera*.

More direct democracy – of better quality

Direct democracy is on the rise, in politics as in showbiz. Our elected representatives must learn to co-exist with it. More than that, they should learn how to harness the energy that popular culture can mobilise. That would mean staying open-minded about experiments like the ITV programme, *Vote for Me*, which allowed viewers to choose a prospective parliamentary candidate. In a nod to the idea that tabloid newspapers express the public mood, one of the judges was Kelvin MacKenzie, former editor of the Sun.

The winner was Rodney Hylton-Potts, who stood on the slogan 'Britain is closed for business'. Hylton-Potts must have made ministers' blood run cold – except that a month later, in February 2005, they unveiled their own plans to restrict immigration by unskilled workers. So he clearly represents a strain of opinion they recognise.

His populist bluster obscured the programme's achievement in giving a platform to people who would not otherwise have thought of entering politics – the other finalists were a campaigner against mobile phone masts, an NHS doctor and a council tenant with ideas for better services on the estate where she lived. There is no reason, other than party protectionism and the design of our electoral system, why they should not stand for Parliament. Television voting is as good a method of selection as a meeting of elderly Conservative association members.

While the media could help clear new routes into politics, the state should assert its pre-eminence in holding the ring and licensing new forms of democratic involvement. Of course newspapers will work any system – it is easy to imagine the *Sun* urging readers to join a signature-collection campaign designed to trigger an official referendum. But they will no longer be able to claim the moral high ground if governments are inviting participation under ground rules that highlight the questionable legitimacy of manufactured dissent.

Experiments with deliberative democracy could help get round the problem of instant, unconsidered reactions. The danger is that Labour has devalued these techniques, through over-use of focus groups and citizens' panels that ended up as window-dressing only. The nationwide consultation on GM served only to create cynicism when it was pointedly ignored.

One answer might be for the Electoral Commission to take on the job of overseeing and monitoring these exercises, to reassure people that the government of the day will not disregard or exploit them for political advantage. Ministers would not be allowed to undertake a consultation or set up a citizens' jury without spelling out what they intended to do with it afterwards. They could be answerable to MPs – through the select committee on public administration or a new committee charged with overseeing participation – for showing what had changed as a result.

Hold the media to account

Politicians find it hard to challenge powerful newspapers on which they depend for coverage and support – although a committed few, like the Labour MPs Clive Soley and Peter Bradley, have campaigned for a right of reply.

The call for Rebekah Wade to be questioned by MPs was a rare attempt to hold a newspaper accountable for its influence. Given that the riots at Paulsgrove did damage and took up police time, it did not seem unreasonable, but the idea was treated as remarkable. She was not, in fact, invited to testify – although later, when editing the *Sun*, she gave evidence to a privacy inquiry by the culture committee.

The episode highlighted the tension between a newspaper's commercial imperative, civic role and partisan mission to represent its own readers. Should Richard Desmond, publisher of the *Daily Express* and the *Daily Star*, be obliged to account for the impact of headlines like 'Immigrant flood is sinking Britain' and 'Asylum: we're being invaded'?[102] As a businessman, his sales figures and bottom line could be justification enough. As a publisher, he knows that the issue worries his readers – and voters in general, judging by the polls.

The trend towards readers' editors and ombudsmen is making newspapers more formally responsive, at least to those who buy them. But there is a distinction between being accountable to readers, which most journalists would support; to politicians, which most would resist; and to the wider community.

At a minimum, the self-regulating Press Complaints Commission should change its rules to allow complaints from third parties, not just the individuals involved. Objections to the *Express*'s coverage of asylum-seekers were rejected because they came from refugee groups and the National Union of Journalists.

Some argue that codes of press conduct should include an explicit duty of 'public disclosure' or 'public responsibility'. The risk is that this could conflict with the duty to protect sources – if, for example, a journalist's duty of public disclosure meant passing information to police. But a media culture that shapes protest needs a sense of the 'public interest' beyond party politics.

Diversify ownership

This old demand, long since dropped from Labour's platform, has some relevance for manufactured dissent. Greater diversity of ownership might have brought balance and sanity to the sometimes hysterical debates over petrol prices, hunting and Section 28. The oligarchy of Fleet Street contrasts with the anarchy of the internet, where new arrivals do not face the start-up costs that barred entry to the newspaper market.

It is worth noticing, however, that different papers within the same group may disagree – the *Sun* and the *News of the World* over naming paedophiles, for example – and that titles from different groups may take the same approach, such as the *Record* and the *Mail* over Section 28.

Equally, the public may not opt for diversity even if offered it. Italians were asked in 1995 if an individual should be prevented from owning more than one television channel, a measure clearly aimed at curbing the power of Silvio Berlusconi. Opponents characterised this as an intolerable restriction of consumer choice, and the result was a 57–43 per cent 'No' vote.

Keep television honest . . .

British television is more closely regulated than the press and maintains its tradition of neutrality. With the rise of cable and satellite channels, that may start to change. In the US, the success of the Murdoch-owned Fox News has revealed an audience for unashamedly partisan coverage.

Television is an important medium for protests – both Sky and BBC News 24 increased their audience during the fuel blockades – so it matters that reporting should be fair and accurate. The pressure for 'light touch' regulation is likely to weaken this commitment to impartiality. At the same time, the demand for irreproachable ethics at the publicly funded BBC – grown louder since the death of Dr David Kelly and the Hutton report – tends to let newspapers off the hook.

. . . and print journalism

An honest and conscientious journalism would try to present the reality of a globalised world where decisions may not be taken at Westminster but in Brussels, the financial markets, or the boardrooms of multinational companies. Where common interests demand trade-offs, such as people using their cars less now to avert floods in future. Where decisions that instinctively seem right, such as letting parents know if a paedophile lives nearby, are examined for unintended consequences.

A glimmer of this is visible in the US movement for 'public' or 'civic' journalism, which holds that journalists should see their role as promoting conversation rather than combat. On this model, newspapers would be more about problem-solving than grandstanding, engaging readers in debates that require something more complex than a yes–no answer.

The idea is, however, fiercely contested by journalists who believe it would replace objectivity with partisanship. It also presumes that civic journalism will shift copies, which, while utterly at odds with conventional wisdom, was the strategy followed by the US tycoons Hearst and Pulitzer in the early years of the twentieth century.[103]

Grown-up politicians

British politics is full of people who are quick to deplore the state of the press yet unwilling to break out of their own formulaic language and solipsistic rituals. Politicians feel trapped by the media, journalists feel caged by 'spin'. Yet they are mutually dependent, and will never be free of the scorpion dance until individuals on both sides are prepared to risk new ways of framing issues and defining public roles. The new journalism would ideally, therefore, be matched by a reformed public life in which politicians occasionally admit to not having the answers and not being in control of events.

Being democrats, these newly realistic representatives would steer constituents in the direction of those who are, thereby offering crash courses in globalisation and multi-layered democracy. Ross Finnie might usefully have led a delegation of anti-GM Highlanders to lobby the European Commission. Labour MPs could have had OPEC's email address on hand during the fuel protests, together with a cribsheet on global warming.

In the hardest cases, there is no single source of authority to point to, but there are links that can be made. Jack McConnell, the First Minister, has been brave enough to make the case that Scotland, with its falling population, should seek to attract immigrant workers – though his room for manoeuvre is circumscribed by the Home Office.

At the micro-level, the Whitehall machine is quietly examining the role of individual responsibility in strategies such as reducing truancy, increasing recycling or cutting car use.[104] Part of grown-up politics is that demands for action should sometimes be bounced back to voters.

Don't confuse spectacle with substance

Protests, if peaceful, appeal to the Lord of Misrule in all of us, bringing theatre and disorder into daily life. That much was obvious from the response to the pro-hunting invasion of the House of Commons in September 2004. For newspapers, a picket or demonstration presents the irresistible combination of good pictures and interviews with 'ordinary' people.

But adrenaline should not obscure reality. The farmers and hauliers who mounted the fuel blockades were given an easy ride by journalists, with several papers using the term 'people's protest'. The Paulsgrove rioters, by contrast, were harshly and sometimes snobbishly characterised as a 'mob' without much attempt to look at why housing policies had placed paedophiles on their estate.

Now that newspapers have become agents and actors in protest movements, the rest of the media must be more alert to the potential for waves of anger to be activated by relatively small groups of people. The Keep the Clause campaign attracted great hostility from other newspapers but less scrutiny of who and what the 'campaign' consisted of. The *Guardian*'s joke team of 'election observers' was the only real effort to examine the *Mail*'s referendum on the European constitution. If protest is being redefined as a picture, a headline and a point of view, it matters more than ever to know who the protesters are, and who the accomplice.

* * *

The intensity with which newspapers are manufacturing dissent denotes panic in the face of falling circulation and the challenge from newer media. The growing use of referenda in the press can be seen as an attempt to mimic the interactive dimensions of television and the internet.

For the market is far from static. Just as parties are out of kilter with abstaining voters, newspapers are seeing their readers drift away. The old class-based marketing strategy is failing: the future lies with more specialist publications, blogs or websites, as consumers construct their own content. For press and politicians, the message is change or die.

The insistence on interactivity reflects a deeper shift. Individualism is intensifying, but so is the demand for agency, as people look for more control over their lives and a say in decisions that affect them.

The press, pursuing readers, has latched on to this trend more quickly than parties: manufactured dissent is one result. Newspapers, in alliance with motley campaigners, are mediating between government and governed, flagging up issues on behalf of a population that will no longer wait to be heard. The axis with protesters is theatrical, sometimes distorted and often irresponsible. But it gives voice to some who might otherwise take the exit route from our democracy.

The trend, while clear, need not be dystopian. Dystopia would be a Berlusconi-style merger of politics and media. The challenge is to find ways in which the interplay of protest, press and politics can be virtuous not vicious in its overall effects.

Notes

1   House of Commons Public Administration Committee, *First Report* (2001).
2   W Lippmann, *Public Opinion* (New York: Macmillan, 1922).
3   E Herman and N Chomsky, *Manufacturing Consent* (New York: Pantheon, 1988).
4   J Nye, *The Paradox of American Power* (Oxford: OUP, 2002).
5   For example, N Klein, *No Logo* (London: Flamingo, 2001) and P Kingsnorth, *One No, Many Yeses* (London: Free Press, 2003). For a critical view, see J Lloyd, *The Protest Ethic* (London: Demos, 2001).
6   D Alexander, 'The new Scottish politics', speech to Progress Scottish Conference, Jun 2003.
7   P Whiteley, 'The state of participation in Britain', *Parliamentary Affairs*, 56 no 4 (2003).
8   P Gundelach, 'Grassroots activity' in JW van Deth and E Scarbrough (eds), *The Impact of Values* (Oxford: Oxford University Press, 1995). The countries studied were Belgium, Britain, Denmark, France, Germany, Iceland, Ireland, Italy, the Netherlands, Norway, Spain and Sweden.
9   S Pattie and P Whiteley, 'Civic attitudes and engagement in modern Britain', *Parliamentary Affairs* 56 no 4 (2003).
10 C Bromley and P Seyd, 'Political engagement, trust and constitutional reform', *British Social Attitudes*, 18th report (2001).
11 W Rudig and C Eschle, 'Who demonstrated on February 15?', (Glasgow: Strathclyde University, 2003).
12 R Dalton, *Democratic Challenges, Democratic Choices* (Oxford, OUP: 2004).
13 A Rawnsley, *Enemies of the People* (London: Penguin, 2001).
14 A Touraine, *Can We Live Together?* (Stanford: Stanford University Press, 1997).
15 *Guardian*, 16 Sep 2004; *Daily Mail*, 16 Sep 2004.
16 P Bourdieu, *On Television* (London: Pluto, 1998).
17 C Horrie, *Tabloid Nation* (London: Deutsch, 2003).
18 *Daily Mail*, 16 Sep 2004; *Guardian*, 16 Sep 2004.
19 S Walgrave and J Menssens, 'The White March: mass media as a mobilizing alternative', *Mobilization* 15 issue 2 (2001).

20   *Eurobarometer* 48 (1998) and 59 (2003).

21   A recent study of UK protests in this period identifies a copycat effect: 'Successful and prominent protest activity by one group fuels the propensity of the general population to protest.' In D Sanders et al, 'The dynamics of protest in Britain 2000–2002', *Parliamentary Affairs* 6, issue 4 (2003).

22   *News of the World*, 16 Jul 2000.

23   *News of the World*, 30 Jul 2000.

24   *Mail on Sunday*, 13 Aug 2000.

25   C Critcher, 'Media, government and moral panic: the politics of paedophilia in Britain 2000–1', *Journalism Studies* 3, no 4 (2002).

26   *Daily Mail*, 11 Aug 2000.

27   *Sunday Times*, 13 Aug 2000; *News of the World*, 20 May 2001.

28   Press Association 12 Dec 2001.

29   *Observer*, 4 Feb 2001.

30   *Scotland on Sunday*, 30 May 2004.

31   Quoted in Rawnsley, *Enemies of the People*.

32   *Evening Standard*, 23 Mar 1999.

33   Rawnsley, *Enemies of the People*.

34   *The Times*, 16 Sep 2000.

35   *Daily Mail*, 9 Sep 2000.

36   *Daily Mail*, 25 Jul 2000.

37   B Doherty et al, 'Explaining the fuel protests', *British Journal of Politics and International Relations*, 5 issue 1 (2003).

38   *Daily Mail*, 13 Sep 2000, 14 Sep 2000 and 12 Sep 2000.

39   *Sun*, 12 Sep 2000; *Daily Mail*, 14 Sep 2000.

40   *Sun*, 14 Sep 2000.

41   *Daily Mail*, 1 Nov; *Sun*, 3 Nov 2000.

42   *Daily Mail*, 9 Nov 2000; *Sun*, 9 Nov 2000.

43   P Kellner, 'The startling truth about the petrol rebels', *Evening Standard*, 10 Oct 2000.

44   See for example 'Greenhouse Britain is heading for catastrophe', *Daily Mail*, 17 Jun 2000.

45   Press Association, 3 Jun 2004.

46   *Hansard*, 20 Jul 2004.

47   *Sun*, 13 Sep 2000.

48   B Doherty et al, 'Explaining the fuel protests'.

49   *Guardian*, 18 Sep 2000.

50   *Guardian*, 22 Feb 2001 and 9 Sep 2002.

51   *Daily Record*, 30 Oct 1999; *Daily Mail*, 30 Oct 1999.

52   *Daily Record*, 16 Dec 1999.

53   'Souter's £1 million to fight gay sex lessons', *Daily Record*, 14 Jan 2000.

54   *Daily Record*, 15 Jan 2000.

55   Private information.

56   For the poll, see *Record*, 8 Mar 2000 and *Daily Mail*, 17 Apr 2000. Both papers carried the legal opinion on 4 Mar 2000 and the *War Cry* story on 7 Apr 2000.

57 *Daily Record*, 2 May 2000 and 13 May 2000.
58 *Sunday Mail*, 7 May 2000 and 30 Apr 2004.
59 *Daily Record*, 12 May 2000, 16 May 2000 and 23 May 2000.
60 Scottish Executive Education Department, *Standards in Scotland's Schools etc.*
    Act 2000: conduct of sex education in Scottish schools (Edinburgh: SEED, 2001).
    Circular 2/2001.
61 Scottish Parliament, *Official Report* 10 Feb 2000, column 938.
62 H Kriesi et al, 'New social movements and political opportunities in western
    Europe', in D McAdam (ed), *Social Movements* (Los Angeles: Roxbury
    Publishing, 1997).
63 Press Association, 11 Nov 2000.
64 *Guardian*, 22 Feb 2001; *Independent*, 27 Sep 2004.
65 *The Times*, 6 Oct 2004 and 13 Apr 2004.
66 *Daily Mail*, 10 Jan 2005.
67 *Daily Mail*, 16 May 2004.
68 R Jenkins, *A Life at the Centre* (London: Macmillan, 1991).
69 *Daily Mail*, 8 May 2003.
70 *Hansard*, 14 May 2003, column 305.
71 *Daily Mail*, 15 May 2003 and 20 May 2003.
72 *Daily Mail*, 29 May 2003.
73 *Daily Mail*, 17 Jun 2003.
74 *Sun*, 20 Apr 2004.
75 *Observer*, 17 Oct 2004.
76 *The Times*, 23 Apr 2004.
77 *Hansard*, 20 Apr 2004, col 156.
78 *Daily Mail*, 20 Jun 2003.
79 *Guardian*, 13 Jun 2003.
80 *Daily Mail*, 11 Jun 2003.
81 ICM State of the Nation poll, Oct 2000, in P Dunleavy (ed), *Voices of the People*
    (London: Politico's Publishing, 2001).
82 *Sunday Herald*, 16 Feb 2003; *Sunday Mirror*, 16 Feb 2003; *Daily Mail*, 17 Feb
    2003; *Independent*, 16 Feb 2003.
83 *Mirror*, 31 Jan 2003.
84 *Liverpool Daily Echo*, 19 Mar 2003.
85 P Schrag, *Paradise Lost: California's experience, America's future* (New York: New
    Press, 1998).
86 S Bowler and T Donovan, 'California's experience with direct democracy',
    Parliamentary Affairs 53 (2000).
87 R Dalton et al, 'Public opinion and direct democracy', *Journal of Democracy*
    (Oct 2001).
88 *Observer*, 25 Apr 2004.
89 Bourdieu, *On Television*.
90 Dunleavy, *Voices of the People*.
91 *Daily Mail*, 8 Oct 2003; *Daily Mail* 26 Nov 2003.
92 On cultural resistance, see Touraine, *Can We Live Together?*; J Habermas, 'New

social movements', *Telos* 49 (1981); Z Bauman, *In Search of Politics* (Cambridge: Polity, 1999). On assertive citizens, see R Inglehart, *Culture Shift in Advanced Industrial Society* (Princeton: Princeton University Press, 1990) and P Norris, *The Democratic Phoenix: reinventing political activism* (Cambridge: Cambridge University Press, 2002).

93 Mori reported in *The Times*, 24 Sep 2002.

94 *Sun*, 24 Sep 2002.

95 Bauman, *In Search of Politics*.

96 M Taylor, 'The future of progressive politics' in G Patmore (ed), *The Vocal Citizen* (Fitzroy, Victoria: Arena, 2004).

97 T Meyer, *Media Democracy* (Cambridge: Polity, 2002); *Guardian*, 17 Jan 2005; J Lloyd, *What the Media Are Doing to Our Politics* (London: Constable, 2004).

98 Mori.com, 'Trust in doctors', 23 Mar 2004; YouGov.com, 'A question of trust', 10 Mar 2003.

99 Lippmann, *Public Opinion*.

100 D Butler et al, *The Politics of the Poll Tax* (Oxford: Oxford University 1994).

101 J Trippi, *The Revolution Will Not Be Televised* (New York: Regan Books, 2004); *Guardian*, 15 Feb 2005.

102 *Daily Star*, 8 Dec 2004; *Daily Express*, 10 Aug 2001.

103 T Glasser (ed), *The Idea of Public Journalism* (New York: Guildford Press, 1999).

104 Prime Minister's Strategy Unit, *Personal Responsibility and Changing Behaviour* (London: Cabinet Office, 2004).

DEMOS – Licence to Publish

THE WORK (AS DEFINED BELOW) IS PROVIDED UNDER THE TERMS OF THIS LICENCE ("LICENCE"). THE WORK IS PROTECTED BY COPYRIGHT AND/OR OTHER APPLICABLE LAW. ANY USE OF THE WORK OTHER THAN AS AUTHORIZED UNDER THIS LICENCE IS PROHIBITED. BY EXERCISING ANY RIGHTS TO THE WORK PROVIDED HERE, YOU ACCEPT AND AGREE TO BE BOUND BY THE TERMS OF THIS LICENCE. DEMOS GRANTS YOU THE RIGHTS CONTAINED HERE IN CONSIDERATION OF YOUR ACCEPTANCE OF SUCH TERMS AND CONDITIONS.

1. **Definitions**
   a **"Collective Work"** means a work, such as a periodical issue, anthology or encyclopedia, in which the Work in its entirety in unmodified form, along with a number of other contributions, constituting separate and independent works in themselves, are assembled into a collective whole. A work that constitutes a Collective Work will not be considered a Derivative Work (as defined below) for the purposes of this Licence.
   b **"Derivative Work"** means a work based upon the Work or upon the Work and other pre-existing works, such as a musical arrangement, dramatization, fictionalization, motion picture version, sound recording, art reproduction, abridgment, condensation, or any other form in which the Work may be recast, transformed, or adapted, except that a work that constitutes a Collective Work or a translation from English into another language will not be considered a Derivative Work for the purpose of this Licence.
   c **"Licensor"** means the individual or entity that offers the Work under the terms of this Licence.
   d **"Original Author"** means the individual or entity who created the Work.
   e **"Work"** means the copyrightable work of authorship offered under the terms of this Licence.
   f **"You"** means an individual or entity exercising rights under this Licence who has not previously violated the terms of this Licence with respect to the Work, or who has received express permission from DEMOS to exercise rights under this Licence despite a previous violation.
2. **Fair Use Rights.** Nothing in this licence is intended to reduce, limit, or restrict any rights arising from fair use, first sale or other limitations on the exclusive rights of the copyright owner under copyright law or other applicable laws.
3. **Licence Grant.** Subject to the terms and conditions of this Licence, Licensor hereby grants You a worldwide, royalty-free, non-exclusive, perpetual (for the duration of the applicable copyright) licence to exercise the rights in the Work as stated below:
   a to reproduce the Work, to incorporate the Work into one or more Collective Works, and to reproduce the Work as incorporated in the Collective Works;
   b to distribute copies or phonorecords of, display publicly, perform publicly, and perform publicly by means of a digital audio transmission the Work including as incorporated in Collective Works;
   The above rights may be exercised in all media and formats whether now known or hereafter devised. The above rights include the right to make such modifications as are technically necessary to exercise the rights in other media and formats. All rights not expressly granted by Licensor are hereby reserved.
4. **Restrictions.** The licence granted in Section 3 above is expressly made subject to and limited by the following restrictions:
   a You may distribute, publicly display, publicly perform, or publicly digitally perform the Work only under the terms of this Licence, and You must include a copy of, or the Uniform Resource Identifier for, this Licence with every copy or phonorecord of the Work You distribute, publicly display, publicly perform, or publicly digitally perform. You may not offer or impose any terms on the Work that alter or restrict the terms of this Licence or the recipients' exercise of the rights granted hereunder. You may not sublicence the Work. You must keep intact all notices that refer to this Licence and to the disclaimer of warranties. You may not distribute, publicly display, publicly perform, or publicly digitally perform the Work with any technological measures that control access or use of the Work in a manner inconsistent with the terms of this Licence Agreement. The above applies to the Work as incorporated in a Collective Work, but this does not require the Collective Work apart from the Work itself to be made subject to the terms of this Licence. If You create a Collective Work, upon notice from any Licencor You must, to the extent practicable, remove from the Collective Work any reference to such Licensor or the Original Author, as requested.
   b You may not exercise any of the rights granted to You in Section 3 above in any manner that is primarily intended for or directed toward commercial advantage or private monetary

compensation. The exchange of the Work for other copyrighted works by means of digital file-sharing or otherwise shall not be considered to be intended for or directed toward commercial advantage or private monetary compensation, provided there is no payment of any monetary compensation in connection with the exchange of copyrighted works.

c If you distribute, publicly display, publicly perform, or publicly digitally perform the Work or any Collective Works, You must keep intact all copyright notices for the Work and give the Original Author credit reasonable to the medium or means You are utilizing by conveying the name (or pseudonym if applicable) of the Original Author if supplied; the title of the Work if supplied. Such credit may be implemented in any reasonable manner; provided, however, that in the case of a Collective Work, at a minimum such credit will appear where any other comparable authorship credit appears and in a manner at least as prominent as such other comparable authorship credit.

5. Representations, Warranties and Disclaimer

a By offering the Work for public release under this Licence, Licensor represents and warrants that, to the best of Licensor's knowledge after reasonable inquiry:

i Licensor has secured all rights in the Work necessary to grant the licence rights hereunder and to permit the lawful exercise of the rights granted hereunder without You having any obligation to pay any royalties, compulsory licence fees, residuals or any other payments;

ii The Work does not infringe the copyright, trademark, publicity rights, common law rights or any other right of any third party or constitute defamation, invasion of privacy or other tortious injury to any third party.

b EXCEPT AS EXPRESSLY STATED IN THIS LICENCE OR OTHERWISE AGREED IN WRITING OR REQUIRED BY APPLICABLE LAW, THE WORK IS LICENCED ON AN "AS IS" BASIS, WITHOUT WARRANTIES OF ANY KIND, EITHER EXPRESS OR IMPLIED INCLUDING, WITHOUT LIMITATION, ANY WARRANTIES REGARDING THE CONTENTS OR ACCURACY OF THE WORK.

6. Limitation on Liability. EXCEPT TO THE EXTENT REQUIRED BY APPLICABLE LAW, AND EXCEPT FOR DAMAGES ARISING FROM LIABILITY TO A THIRD PARTY RESULTING FROM BREACH OF THE WARRANTIES IN SECTION 5, IN NO EVENT WILL LICENSOR BE LIABLE TO YOU ON ANY LEGAL THEORY FOR ANY SPECIAL, INCIDENTAL, CONSEQUENTIAL, PUNITIVE OR EXEMPLARY DAMAGES ARISING OUT OF THIS LICENCE OR THE USE OF THE WORK, EVEN IF LICENSOR HAS BEEN ADVISED OF THE POSSIBILITY OF SUCH DAMAGES.

7. Termination

a This Licence and the rights granted hereunder will terminate automatically upon any breach by You of the terms of this Licence. Individuals or entities who have received Collective Works from You under this Licence, however, will not have their licences terminated provided such individuals or entities remain in full compliance with those licences. Sections 1, 2, 5, 6, 7, and 8 will survive any termination of this Licence.

b Subject to the above terms and conditions, the licence granted here is perpetual (for the duration of the applicable copyright in the Work). Notwithstanding the above, Licensor reserves the right to release the Work under different licence terms or to stop distributing the Work at any time; provided, however that any such election will not serve to withdraw this Licence (or any other licence that has been, or is required to be, granted under the terms of this Licence), and this Licence will continue in full force and effect unless terminated as stated above.

8. Miscellaneous

a Each time You distribute or publicly digitally perform the Work or a Collective Work, DEMOS offers to the recipient a licence to the Work on the same terms and conditions as the licence granted to You under this Licence.

b If any provision of this Licence is invalid or unenforceable under applicable law, it shall not affect the validity or enforceability of the remainder of the terms of this Licence, and without further action by the parties to this agreement, such provision shall be reformed to the minimum extent necessary to make such provision valid and enforceable.

c No term or provision of this Licence shall be deemed waived and no breach consented to unless such waiver or consent shall be in writing and signed by the party to be charged with such waiver or consent.

d This Licence constitutes the entire agreement between the parties with respect to the Work licensed here. There are no understandings, agreements or representations with respect to the Work not specified here. Licensor shall not be bound by any additional provisions that may appear in any communication from You. This Licence may not be modified without the mutual written agreement of DEMOS and You.